in

Rhode Island

40 Trails for Birders and Nature Lovers

The surf and bluffs help make Block Island irresistible.

in

Rhode Island

40 Trails for Birders and Nature Lovers

THIRD EDITION

KEN WEBER

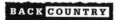

Backcountry Guides
Woodstock, Vermont

An Invitation to the Reader

If you find that conditions have changed along these walks, please let the author and publisher know so that corrections may be made in future editions. Address all correspondence to:

Editor
Walks & Rambles Series
The Countryman Press
PO Box 748
Woodstock, Vermont 05091

Library of Congress Cataloging-in-Publication Data

Weber, Ken
    Walks and rambles in Rhode Island : 40 trails for birders and nature lovers / Ken Weber. — 3rd ed.
        p.   cm.
    ISBN 0-88150-458-0 (paper)
        1. Hiking—Rhode Island—Guidebooks. 2. Rhode Island—Guidebooks. I. Title.
GV199.42.R4W44 1999
917.4504'43—dc21   98-52037
                                                                                    CIP

Published by Backcountry Guides
A division of The Countryman Press, PO Box 748, Woodstock, VT 05091
Distributed by W. W. Norton & Company, Inc., 500 Fifth Avenue, New York, NY 10110
Printed in the United States of America
Text and cover design by Sally Sherman
Maps and calligraphy by Alex Wallach and Jacques Chazaud
Photographs by the author
Printed in the United States of America
10 9 8 7 6 5 4 3 2

For all the men, women, and children who enjoy exploring Rhode Island on foot, and especially for those who work to preserve and improve our trails.

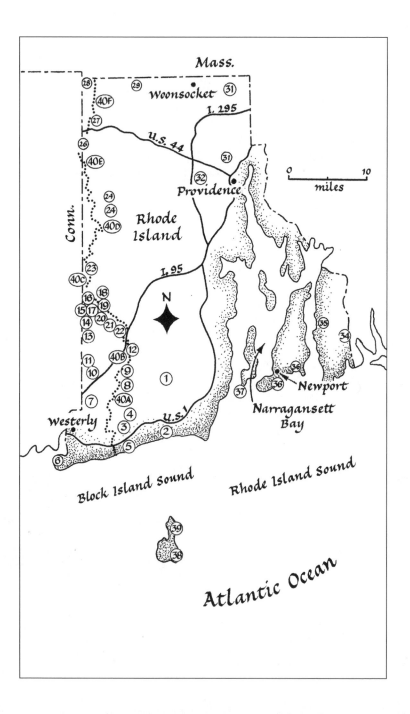

Contents

Acknowledgments

Walking is more enjoyable with congenial companions, and I want to thank those who frequently joined me on the trails, starting with my wife, Bettie Weber. Other friends and walking partners were Joe Healey, Marie Fontaine, Judy Garthwaite, Steve Garthwaite, Guy Latour, and Jack Hilton. Each brought new perspectives as well as camaraderie to the walks. Also of significant help were David Rodrigues, of the Audubon Society of Rhode Island; Ginger Carpenter and Scott Comings, of The Nature Conservancy; Jay Aron and Brian Tefft, of the Rhode Island Department of Environmental Management; and Ginny Leslie, of the North South Trail Council. I thank all of them.

Introduction

It was more than 25 years ago when I began walking Rhode Island trails, and more than 20 years ago when my first guide to trails, *25 Walks in Rhode Island,* was published. Much has changed in that time, most of it for the better.

This third edition of *Walks and Rambles in Rhode Island* details many of the changes, and will bring some new trails to the attention of hikers. I've spent the last year rewalking all 40 of the trails that were included in the second edition of *Walks and Rambles,* and updating those routes that I wanted to retain for this edition. However, in exploring new territory, I came across several trails not included before, so there has been considerable revising. For example, a new property opened by the Audubon Society of Rhode Island in North Smithfield is now included, along with a new property of The Nature Conservancy in Richmond and state management areas in Hopkinton and Little Compton that had not been detailed previously. I've also added a walk in the Burlingame Management Area in Charlestown, which could be linked to a cherished old trail in nearby Burlingame State Park.

And for the 40th walk, I'm including the 77-mile North South Trail that runs the length of the state, along its western edge, from the ocean at Charlestown to the Massachusetts line above Burrillville. Obviously, with a trail that long I cannot go into nearly as much detail as I do on other walks, but I've tried to provide key information throughout its route. The North South incorporates into its system many other trails that are covered in detail in both this book and its companion, *More Walks and Rambles in Rhode Island,* so walkers should get an adequate picture of the route, which has been several years in the making.

In adding all of these walks, I've dropped others for various reasons: They have deteriorated or been changed in a less-than-desirable manner, or, in my opinion, they are no longer as interesting as the new walks.

This lane invites walkers to explore the center of Block Island.

I've found that virtually every trail has changed to some extent. But this is normal with hiking routes. Sometimes landmark trees blow down. Sometimes beavers flood areas and new routes must be devised. Sometimes trails are extended or shortened for other reasons. Sometimes the changes involve nothing more than a different color of blazes, or a new place to park. With these walks the overwhelming majority of changes have been positive. And just the fact that changes do occur can be good for hikers. It means that walking the trails never becomes stale. Time and again over the last year, when walking paths that I've been on a dozen times, I found myself marveling over rock ledges or tranquil little ponds or surging young pine groves, all features that were present years ago but now look different, because either they have changed or their surroundings have.

The walks are again arranged geographically, starting with one of the state's unique places, the Great Swamp, and then going clockwise around the southwestern, western, northern, and eastern areas before featuring another special place, Block Island. I saved the North South Trail for the end.

Most of the walks are loops that enable you to return to the point where you began without backtracking. Some, however, are one-way walks that require leaving another car at your destination. It is important that you read the descriptions before starting out in order to best prepare yourself. The descriptions tell you not only how long the walk is in both miles and time, but also how difficult it may be and what you are likely to see along the way. I've also tried to recommend the best times of year for each walk and whether the trails link with other paths, and thereby can be extended or shortened.

Approximate walking times are subjective; many hikers could do these walks in far less time than listed. But I don't consider walking a competitive sport or an endurance event. Those who plunge ahead—never stopping, looking neither left nor right—miss far too much. There is so much beauty, history, and wildlife along these routes that it would be a shame not to see as much as possible, and that takes a little slowing down and some occasional stops.

Sketch maps of each walk are included to help you visualize the described route. The following standard map symbols are used:

Ⓟ	parking area
●●●●	main trail
· · · ·	side trail or alternate route
X	point of interest
▨	fields
⚓ ⚓	marsh
■	building
⋈	bridge
†	cemetery
♠	church
⚜	tower (observation, water, etc.)
⚓ ⚓	ferry
⚱	lighthouse
▮	boat ramp

Those who would like more detailed maps should obtain US Geological Survey topographic sheets, available at many sporting goods stores. In addition, the Rhode Island Department of Environmental Management prints maps of its management areas, and both The Nature Conservancy and the Audubon Society of Rhode Island can provide maps of their properties that are open to the public.

Revising this book for a third edition gave me a good chance to gauge where Rhode Island hiking is going. Simply having so many trails to choose from shows that more land is being protected and set aside for public enjoyment. And as I wrote when preparing the previous edition, I found myself getting excited all over again about Rhode Island's walking places. If you haven't been on these paths before, you're in for a treat. If you're walking them again after not having seen them for a few years, I think you'll relish the experience. Walking Rhode Island continues to get better.

Great Swamp

A walk around a wildlife marsh to see holly trees, ospreys, and waterfowl

Hiking distance: 5½ miles
Hiking time: 3–3½ hours
Difficulty: Easy; flat, open lanes all the way

One of the reasons for choosing one walk over another is the chance to see something different. At the Great Swamp in South Kingstown, you'll see several things not normally found elsewhere, particularly holly trees and ospreys.

There are not many places more interesting for those who see hiking as more than mere walking. The route described here is an easy 5½-mile loop that runs through dense woodland, visits a large pond and a World War II–era airplane hangar, then wanders by management fields and follows a dike around an intriguing wildlife marsh. For those who so desire, a walk at least partway into the marsh is possible on a boardwalk that runs under power-line poles on which ospreys nest. The entire route could be walked in a couple of hours but it usually takes much longer—there are so many reasons to stop and linger.

The 3,000-acre Great Swamp is one of the state management areas that cater to sportspeople, but in doing so it also contributes immensely to the proliferation of wildlife. Once, this area was the last stronghold of Rhode Island's Native Americans; now it is home to many plants and animals that have been decimated elsewhere in the state.

The best time to make this walk is in spring, when migrating songbirds fill the bushes; ducks, geese, and other waterbirds are nesting in the marsh; and ospreys are returning to nests atop the poles.

©1999 The Countryman Press

Bring along binoculars and perhaps a camera with a telephoto lens. The lanes are open in other seasons as well, and each time of year has its charm here, but remember that the swamp teems with hunters in late autumn and early winter.

Access

To reach the Great Swamp, take RI 138 to the village of West Kingston, turn west (a sign points the way) onto Liberty Lane, and follow the road just under a mile until it ends at a railroad track. Then go left onto a gravel lane about 1 mile, passing office and maintenance buildings, and park in an open lot at a barred gateway.

Trail

You will walk on access roads throughout this hike. The woods are both damp and dense, in some areas nearly impenetrable. But there is no need to leave the roads; you can see so much from the flat, open lanes.

Tall trees shade the road at the start, and the understory of young dogwoods, blueberry bushes, blackberries, and pepperbushes adds colorful variety. In spring you are likely to see violets beside the road; in summer there will be pretty purple flowers called deer grass; and in winter the bright red berries of the black alder practically glow against the stark background. Autumn, of course, has the showy foliage. On spring walks you can expect to see and hear catbirds, towhees, orioles, ovenbirds, and numerous species of warblers along this route. When you reach the marsh, waterfowl, ospreys, and swallows take over.

In less than ½ mile the road splits at a marker honoring Dr. John Mulleedy, a late hiking club leader. If you want to see only the marsh, you can take the right fork. For this walk, however, keep to the left. You will be returning on the other path.

The feature of this next section is the holly. These trees, so eagerly sought at Christmastime, are abundant along this road; you can probably find more here than anywhere else in the state. Look but don't touch—they're protected by law. They are especially vibrant in winter, when red berries embellish the shiny green foliage, but they also stand out in early spring, before the surrounding trees and bushes open their leaves.

After crossing a clearing cut for the power line (a path to the right leads to the marsh), you enter a drier forest rich with ferns. Without leaving the road you can find ferns of half a dozen varieties. Mixed in are creeping jenny and princess pine, two club mosses also protected by law. And guarding the plants, in many places, are thorny brambles of greenbrier.

At the next major junction, you'll find another granite marker, this one memorializing George McCahey, also a prominent hiker of years past. Again, take the left fork, and remain on this lane as it passes

For many, the ospreys are the best reason to visit Great Swamp.

several narrow cutoff paths. This area is dotted with large boulders and low ledges. In less than ½ mile from the McCahey marker, the lane ends at the old seaplane hangar at the edge of Worden Pond. As you approach the hangar, take note of a narrow path going off to the right in front of the building; you'll be leaving via this trail.

But take some time to look over the hangar and the shallow, 1,000-acre pond. The view from here is terrific, and chances are good you'll see more birds, perhaps kingfishers, ducks, swans, and many others. There also have been beavers in this area, off and on, in recent years, and you may see their telltale sign of chewed-off saplings.

When you are ready to resume walking, take the narrow path away from the hangar. It is very narrow at first, and may be boggy, but in a short distance the path opens and the walking is again easy and pleasant. Now, however, the going gets a little tricky because the lane curls along and beside numerous small fields planted in grain for wildlife or left as meadows, and each has an entrance that can be mistaken for a roadway. As a general rule, stay on the widest, most-used lane. Usually (but not always), you are making left turns at forks, but if you remain on the wider lane, you should have no trouble.

In about ½ mile from the hangar, you will emerge on a gravel road. Turn left, downhill, and in a few minutes you will reach the marsh. The road runs the length of the dike built in the 1950s to create the 140-acre marsh.

This may be the best segment of the entire walk, especially for those who like birds. Numerous wood-duck boxes dot the marsh, and swimming among the water lilies and other aquatic plants are usually ducks, swans, and geese. Herons and kingfishers are common, too, and swallows fill the air (and most of the duck houses).

More likely to capture your attention, however, are the ospreys, the big, fish-eating hawks once close to extinction in Rhode Island. To the right you can see the string of power-line poles across the marsh, and balanced atop many of the poles are the ospreys' bulky nests. No other place in the state has as many ospreys as the Great Swamp, and the grassy dike and the boardwalk beneath the poles offer superb places to sit and watch the graceful birds, and perhaps try photographing them. It's likely there will be other photographers here, particularly in spring, when the ospreys are adding sticks to those huge nests.

Along the left side of the curving dike is shallow water that features turtles, frogs, and wildflowers. Beyond the stream is a junglelike tangle of dense undergrowth. Chances are you'll find deer tracks on the dike, and once my wife and I saw a beautiful young buck running full speed toward us here. He came within a few yards before veering off.

The dike is more than a mile long, and the views are good all the way. Just before the end of the dike, you can see a beaver lodge off to your right. Beyond are two more poles put up for ospreys but unused at present. When they are in use, they present excellent opportunities for pictures because there are no wires, as is the case at the power-line nests.

Shortly after the lane returns to the woods, you reach an intersection of paths. Go left. You'll follow the power line briefly, then walk beside an open field that is likely to hold more birds, before joining the main entrance road at the Mulleedy marker. A left turn takes you back to the parking lot.

Trustom Pond

A superb birding walk through a former farm to a coastal sanctuary

Hiking distance: 3 miles
Hiking time: 1½–2 hours
Difficulty: Easy; the entire route is on flat, open paths

Trustom Pond is for the birds—and that's the way the people who manage the place want it. On this walk, you will see a great variety of birds and will note just how much effort has been put into making this coastal sanctuary appealing to them.

Trustom Pond National Wildlife Refuge encompasses far more than the saltwater pond of its name. The refuge also takes in what once was a farm, and the trails run along open fields, through abandoned pastures now being reclaimed by forest, and past low-lying marshes. You can visit each terrain on this 3-mile walk and, as a bonus, look at a windmill left over from the days when this was a thriving sheep farm belonging to the Alfred Morse family, who eventually donated the property to the US Fish and Wildlife Service.

Throughout the area, there are birdhouses and nesting aids for birds ranging from ospreys to bluebirds to wood ducks. On a good day, perhaps a sunny morning in May, you might find as many as 40 or 50 species of birds on this easy, comfortable ramble. To help birders, observation towers have been built at several strategic points, and this refuge has an additional attraction: A handicapped-accessible trail runs from the parking lot to a small pond and a wooden observation deck.

Access

To reach the refuge, take US 1 in South Kingstown to Moonstone Beach Road. Follow that road south 1 mile and turn right onto Matunuck Schoolhouse Road. The refuge entrance is 0.7 mile on the left.

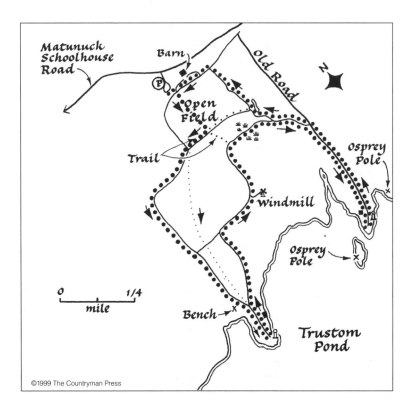

Matunuck
Schoolhouse
Road

Barn

Old Road

N

Open
Field

Trail

Osprey
Pole

Windmill

Osprey
Pole

0   1/4
    mile

Bench

Trustom
Pond

Trail

From the parking lot, a walkway leads first to a kiosk, which describes the sanctuary and outlines the trails: the Osprey Point Trail and the Rolling Meadows Trail. On the walk described here, you'll travel both paths.

Your birding begins immediately. On the short stroll to the trails' starting points, you pass through a thicket of bushes where you are likely to find warblers, catbirds, towhees, thrashers, and other songbirds. When you emerge into an open field, look for bluebirds, swallows, bobolinks, meadowlarks, and perhaps a hunting marsh hawk.

The trail to the left is the path accessible to wheelchairs. It runs to the pond, which may have wood ducks and almost always, in warm

weather, contains turtles, frogs, dragonflies, and similar pond creatures. That path is part of the Rolling Meadows Trail and, unless the
pond is your prime objective, will be your return route.

Follow the trail that cuts straight across the open field. This is
the Osprey Point Trail. It is marked with signs and arrows and is easy
to follow.

After crossing the open field, the Osprey Point Trail splits. You
can continue straight ahead through the next section or turn to the
right, following a stone wall. That is the way I prefer, simply to add
a little more distance to the walk. Both legs run through similar areas
filled with bushes and small trees. There are a great many wild berries
growing here—blueberries, raspberries, wild cherries, and viburnums;
consequently, birds are usually abundant. Robins, catbirds, jays, orioles,
and many, many others congregate here in summer. You're also likely
to see deer tracks, or the deer themselves, in this area.

Where the trail meets another path coming in from the left, you
will see a wooden bench. You will eventually take this other path, but
first follow the main lane out onto a point that reaches into Trustom
Pond. Usually, there are terns, geese, ducks, and swans on the pond.
An observation deck provides good views to the left, and on that side
you can see a small island on which a pole and a platform have been
installed for ospreys. The platform nest is often in use and you may
want to linger here, watching these graceful fish hawks.

At the very tip of the point is another observation tower, and
there is much to see. Many forms of waterfowl rest on the pond during migration flights, and songbirds also congregate in this area in
spring and fall. One birder recently identified 46 species from this
tower in one October day. The sand dune across the pond, Moonstone Beach, is also a bird refuge.

When you are ready to resume walking, go back up the trail to
the fork at the bench. The cutoff, now on your right, is narrow and
winding but easy to walk. It runs through another thicket of small
trees, including some apples, and follows a stone wall briefly before
reaching a grassy lane. Take this lane to the right.

Now you are entering an area used as a sheep pasture shortly
before the land became a refuge. The sheep barn formerly stood just

Observation towers aid birders at Trustom Pond.

to your right, on the opposite side of the stone wall. Now the entire area is quickly reverting to forest.

Pass an open path to the left (it is the alternate route from the open field) and continue following the lane to the point where it turns left near taller trees. Off the trail, to the right, you can see the windmill, perhaps the last reminder of the sheep, other than the stone walls. The windmill, several yards off the trail, in the shadow of tall trees, no longer pumps water but the blades still spin in the breeze, adding an idyllic touch to the scene.

From the windmill, follow the open trail as it runs through young forest until it forks. Going left would take you back to the open field you crossed earlier. But go to the right for the walk on the Rolling Meadows Trail.

You'll go through a dense, damp thicket, crossing the wettest area on a wooden walkway, then pass a side trail on the left. You will walk this side path later, but for now, continue straight ahead to an old road that follows a line of trees and still another stone wall. Turn right onto this shady, picturesque road and follow it out to a second point in Trustom Pond.

This point is lovely indeed, with sea breezes, more birds, and more pond views. Until a few years ago, the Morses' cabin stood here, adding another pleasing touch, but it was removed because of vandalism. Now only a pump, a tiny shed, and a few relic apple trees remain from the family retreat.

At the point, benches and an observation tower make the birding easy and comfortable. A second osprey pole stands on the left, and the shallow water to the right of the point is a haven for shorebirds as well as larger waterfowl.

When you return up the old road, take the path (now on your left) that you walked earlier, then take the cutoff to the right just before the damp thicket. This trail curls around a small pond equipped with a pier, an observation deck, wood-duck houses, and a purple martin house. Whether you see wood ducks or not, you are fairly sure to see turtles and frogs.

Beyond the pond, follow the wheelchair-accessible trail as it runs along the open field and then turns left. You'll be passing the refuge maintenance buildings, on your right. This lane will take you to the trailhead and the thicket you walked through when you left the kiosk. Chances are, the warblers and catbirds will still be there, waiting for you.

Vin Gormley Trail

A long stroll through lovely woods, over little brooks, and past rocky ledges

Hiking distance: 8¼ miles
Hiking time: 3½–4 hours
Difficulty: Long but fairly easy; segments on
roads, minor ups and downs

This long trail, around Watchaug Pond in Burlingame State Park in Charlestown, is meant for slow, contemplative strolling. It's fairly easy, and while not spectacular, it offers a good variety of attractions, from the large pond itself to damp lowlands, from rugged rock ledges to lively little brooks and streams.

Renamed for John Vincent "Vin" Gormley, who maintained the trail well into his 80s, the trail also breaks out onto roads at times, which can be either a blessing or a curse, depending on your perspective. It runs through both a quiet wildlife sanctuary and a busy campground, but most of this walk is in forest. The trail is well used, well blazed, and well maintained. Still, while the bright yellow blazes are easy to follow, some care must be taken because the trail joins and leaves other lanes and paths many times. So don't spend all your time admiring the trees; keep one eye on the yellow marks, particularly the double blazes, which in the Appalachian Mountain Club system indicate changes of direction.

I suggest making this walk in spring or fall. Autumn walks are colorful because of the abundance of hardwood trees, but spring might be even better because seasonal brooks add a flair (and a degree of muddy footing) that includes a couple of minor waterfalls in the second half of the walk.

Access

Except for the section that includes paved roads, the entire trail is within Burlingame State Park, so the best starting place is the picnic

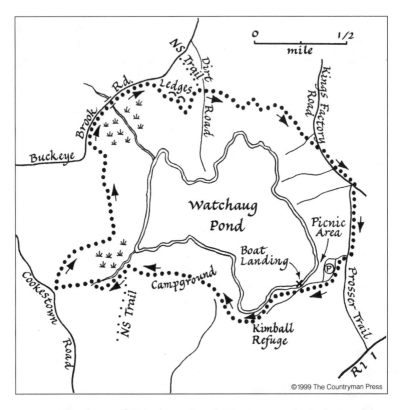

area on the shore of Watchaug Pond. Here, not only is there a large parking area, but also walkers can use the tables for a post-walk lunch and maybe take a swim.

Drive RI 1 southbound west of RI 2 and RI 112, following signs for Burlingame Park, until you reach a paved road called Prosser Trail. Turn right onto Prosser and go 0.6 mile to the park entrance on your left. Immediately, you should see the yellow blazes for the Gormley Trail, which follows this entrance into the park and runs along the outer edge of the parking lot.

Trail

You can walk either way around the pond, but for this walk, begin by going left. The road passes a string of houses and the park's boat ramp before entering the Kimball Wildlife Refuge, an Audubon Society sanctuary that is a favorite spot for area birders. Immediately upon entering the refuge, the yellow trail leaves the roadway and breaks off to the right.

In this section, the trail runs closer to the 900-acre pond than at any other point in your walk, and you can take side trails to the water's edge. You'll see paths blazed in other colors here, too—they are part of the Kimball trail system—so be sure to return to the yellow trail if you wander off.

You will be in the refuge only briefly before breaking into the Burlingame Camping Area, the state's largest public campground, less than 1 mile from your start. Because the trail cuts directly through the campground, you may have to look closely to see the blazes. You enter between the camp store, on your left, and a playground area. In summer, this is a bustling little city of camp vehicles and tents. You'll walk some paved roads and cross a couple of traffic islands before leaving the campground on a grassy lane, beside a HIKERS ONLY sign between campsites 493 and 494.

Now you are entering dense, damp forest, but the trail remains wide and easy to walk. In minutes, the yellow blazes are joined by blue markers, because the long North South Trail (Walk 40) comes in from the left. For the next 4 miles, you'll be following both yellow and blue blazes.

Where the trail makes an abrupt turn left, you are making the detour around the swampy area formerly crossed by a walkway. The old walkway, which carried hikers above the swamp, was a favored feature years ago. When it deteriorated, though, replacing it was deemed too costly. Now the trail, after turning left, winds through thick stands of mountain laurel and other bushes, passes stone walls, and crosses brooks on log bridges and short walkways. It can be muddy in places.

Just as you seem about to emerge on a gravel road (Cookestown Road), roughly 2½ miles into your walk, the trail makes a sharp right turn beside a stone wall and remains in forest. This leads to an attractive segment that features a mixture of pines and hardwoods accented with boulders and brooks. In about ⅓ mile from the gravel-

The Vin Gormley Trail wanders for miles through dense forest.

road turn, you make a 90-degree turn left (the path to the right is the old swamp trail). Now you are on an open lane flanked by delightful trees and stone walls, a stretch particularly inviting in autumn. You follow this lane for about ½ mile, then the yellow-blue trail turns off to the right. Be sure to make this turn (it is well marked), because the lane would lead you astray.

For the next mile, the trail curves around through farmland-returned-to-forest, as evidenced by the many lanes and stone walls. Your path joins and leaves the larger lanes, so you again have to pay attention to the yellow and blue blazes. When the trail emerges onto a paved road, you are on Buckeye Brook Road. Take it to the right. You'll pass a swampy area and cross a stream, but your stay on the pavement is only ¼ mile before returning to the woods on the right.

Now you are descending into a beech grove that shades the largest ledges along the trail. You walk at the base of the jagged glacial rocks, but can take side paths to the tops of several of the little cliffs. These ledges are approximately 5 miles into your walk and a great place to rest and linger awhile.

Beyond the ledges, the trail is very curvy as it gradually climbs away from the unseen pond, and it is in this area that the blue North South Trail finally leaves the yellow trail, turning left at a T-intersection and going out to Buckeye Brook Road and the Burlingame North Trail (Walk 4). The yellow trail, again labeled HIKERS ONLY, (although tire tracks show other users), crosses a short log walkway, then reaches a private gravel road. You cross the road and walk through a rocky section laced with brooks. Again, from time to time, you follow old lanes briefly, and at one point, shortly after passing the gravel road, you cross a little brook that, in spring, cascades into a lovely falls just to the right of your path. Farther ahead, about 6½ miles into your walk, you reach another spot where a spring brook sweeps directly over the large table rock that is part of the trail. This is another good place for a pause, and a bench has been installed here for that purpose. Both of these small waterfalls dry up in summer.

The trail crosses another private roadway about ½ mile beyond the falls and bench, and immediately returns to forest behind a house. In minutes, you break out of the woods for the final time onto a paved road. This is Kings Factory Road. The yellow blazes turn right for the return to Watchaug Pond. You follow Kings Factory Road about ⅓ mile to the first intersection, then go right onto Prosser Trail about ½ mile to the park entrance, the picnic area, and your car.

Burlingame North

A slow woods stroll past stone walls and stone dams to a camping area along a river

Hiking distance: 4 miles
Hiking time: 2½–3 hours
Difficulty: Easy; old roads nearly all the way

This area, the Burlingame Wildlife Management Area, is not nearly as well known as adjoining Burlingame State Park and the Vin Gormley Trail (Walk 3), but it is a gem in its own right. It is a terrific place to walk in all seasons, but especially inviting in spring, when the brooks are running fast and the birds are back to serenade you.

There are no formal hiking trails in this 1,390-acre area, but a network of old roads enables visitors to make their own loops. The entry road is blazed in blue because it is part of the North South Trail (Walk 40), and the only segment of the recommended route not on open lanes is blazed in white, so there is little chance of losing your way.

Attractions here, in addition to the bird life and the variety of trees, include two high stone dams left over from an earlier era; an earthen dam and the pond it created; many stone walls that wander all over the forest; ledges and rock outcroppings; and, if you make the full 4-mile circuit, a visit to a canoe campground on the banks of the Pawcatuck River.

Since this section of Burlingame is a management area, it is open to hunters in late fall and winter. Anyone using the property at that time must wear fluorescent orange. Spring may be a better time to visit.

Access

Take RI 216 in Charlestown to Buckeye Brook Road, turn east, and follow Buckeye Brook Road 1.9 miles to a marked parking area on the north (left) side of the road.

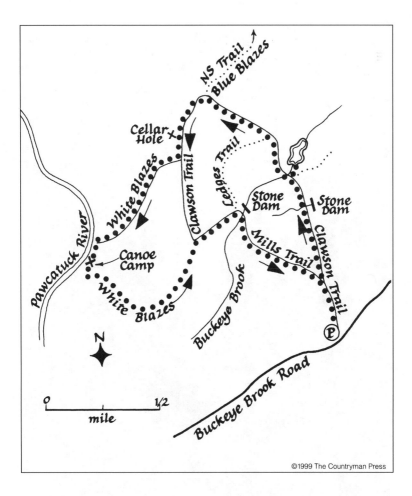

©1999 The Countryman Press

Trail

Pines shade the first segment of the entrance road, identified on state management maps as Clawson Trail. You will be following the blue blazes of the North South Trail, which crosses Buckeye Brook Road from Burlingame Park. Here you'll also see the first of many outcroppings, on your right, and the first of even more stone walls, also on the right. There is virtually no time on this walk when you are out of sight of stone walls.

Old stone dams are a feature of the Burlingame North Trail.

At a Y-junction, about ⅓ mile from your start, follow the blue NST blazes to the right. Now there is more variety in the forest, with hemlocks and many species of hardwoods along the road in addition to pines. Not far beyond the fork you'll see, on the right, one of the old stone dams. Once the dam created a pond; now, very little water gathers behind it.

At the next junction, however, where a lane labeled BURDICK TRAIL branches off to the right, you can see, just ahead and to the right, an earthen dam that is still in use. Take the grassy path to the dike. The impounded water often hosts waterbirds (there are two nesting boxes for wood ducks), and otters are seen here occasionally. The stream dammed here is Buckeye Brook, for which the paved road was named. This spot is about ¾ mile into your walk.

Back on the main trail, you'll pass several seasonal pools, which in spring may reverberate with the calling of frogs. The lane curves considerably, weaving around the hollows and outcroppings. At 1⅓ miles, you reach another lane going to the left. This one, Ledges Trail, can be used as a shortcut if desired. Flanked by outcroppings, it curls through the forest and joins Mills Trail, which you can take back toward the parking area. However, making that choice would mean missing some of the area's highlights.

Instead, stay on Clawson Trail and the blue blazes. However, at the next fork the blue blazes turn right and soon leave state property. Now go to the left on the wider lane, still Clawson Trail. This is a particularly inviting segment with tall trees, stone walls on both sides, and a wide, easy-to-walk lane. Deer tracks and sign of wild turkeys are common here, and in spring you may see a few brave blossoms on the remnant apple trees in a long-abandoned orchard on the right. Just beyond this orchard, buried in a tangle of vines and briers, is the cellar hole of a vanished home.

The next point to look for, about ¼ mile from the turn where you left the blue blazes, is a lane going to the right. It is marked with white blazes and a sign saying RIVER LOOP. Take this detour; it goes to the river and canoe camp. The ½-mile walk to the river runs mostly downhill through dense brush that offers excellent birding in spring. The lane emerges in a clearing just above a bend in the wide Pawcatuck,

beside the foundation of what was a large building. This is where canoeists pull ashore and camp.

The white-blazed trail runs behind the camping area, but I suggest leaving it for a path along the water's edge. This path, which
links the various campsites, offers several good views of the river as
it climbs a knoll in a pine grove. In summer, this campground is often
filled, particularly on weekends, but in spring it can be a good place
to look, listen, and linger.

When you are ready to resume walking, return to the white-
blazed trail. The lane it was following ends at the campground, but
the trail goes on as a footpath. It weaves through the woods, skirting
a low, damp area, then gradually makes its way uphill through forest
that features boulders and stone walls. This footpath segment, about
¾ mile long, emerges on the old road marked MILLS TRAIL.

Taking the road to the right, you walk beneath towering oaks
for about ⅓ mile until Ledges Trail joins you from the left. Just
beyond this junction, you cross Buckeye Brook again. On the left is
the second high stone dam, and it is worth inspecting. Reinforced and
reshaped with cement in the 1940s, the open gate forms a picturesque
waterfall in spring when the brook is running high. It is another
pretty spot where lingering is easy.

From the dam, the road runs just over ½ mile, passing through
a grove of dead pines, before ending at Clawson Trail. Turn right for
the return to your car.

Ninigret Beach

A 6-mile beach walk with a wide variety of ocean birds and seashore plants

Hiking distance: 6 miles
Hiking time: 3 hours
Difficulty: Easy, although
a bit tiring; all in sand

The long miles of beach and sand in the Ninigret Conservation Area of Charlestown offer extremes in weather and walking conditions. In cold, windy weather it can be a desolate place of icy blasts. But in mild, sunny weather it can be one of the best places around Rhode Island for a seashore walk. The beach is open, clean, and, except during summer, virtually empty of other people.

People walk beaches for many reasons, but one of the best reasons for visiting Ninigret is the abundance of birds you are likely to see riding the waves just offshore. Go in early spring—March or April—before the wintering waterfowl have returned north, and you may see dozens of birds of several varieties.

Ninigret stretches 3 miles to a breachway, so a walk the length of the beach and back is 6 miles. For a change of pace and scenery, you could also return by way of a sand road up on the dune that separates the ocean from Ninigret Pond, a large, shallow salt pond known for its crabs, clams, and other aquatic life. Returning on the sand road, which would add about ½ mile to your walk, allows you to see more of the plants of the seashore, along with the songbirds that inhabit the bushes, but walking that road is extremely tiring. I suggest returning on the beach, then going through the parking lot to the pond for a look at its wildlife and plants.

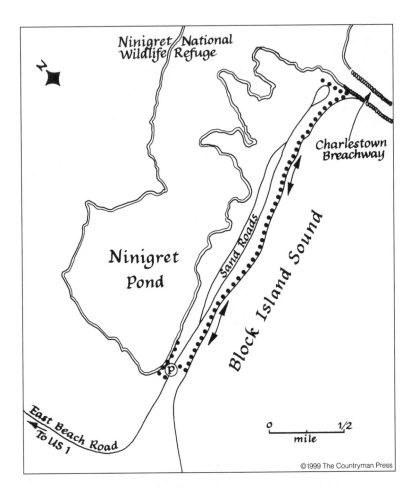

As a barrier beach, Ninigret is the first line of defense against storms that sweep in from Block Island Sound, and therefore is very important to the coastline and Ninigret Pond. For that reason, please obey all signs regarding the fragile dunes.

Access

The only road to the conservation area (not to be confused with the more visible Ninigret National Wildlife Refuge, on the north side of Ninigret Pond, accessible from US 1) is East Beach Road. It also is reached via US 1, just east of RI 216. Follow East Beach Road until its end at the shore, then go left onto a gravel road, past numerous cottages, until you see the conservation area sign and parking lot. If you go in summer, be sure to arrive early; the parking area fills quickly with swimmers and sunbathers. From Memorial Day to Labor Day, here is a fee for parking. In the off-season, entry is free.

Trail

From the parking lot, use the designated crossing over the ridge of sand to the shore and begin walking east (to your left). In swimming season, this first section is likely to be jammed, but proceed to the edge of the water, where the firm sand is much easier to walk on, and begin. In a matter of minutes you will be beyond the crowds, and after that you will meet only occasional walkers, joggers, and surf fishermen. In the off-season, you may have the entire beach to yourself, although occasionally Jeeps, dune buggies, and other recreational vehicles run along the beach.

On a clear day you can see Block Island, which lies about 12 miles offshore. It seems much closer, but distances over water can be deceiving. For instance, as you look east down the beach, you can easily make out the dark line of Charlestown Breachway extending into the water. The line is a mass of large rocks and appears a relatively short stroll away. Those rocks are, in fact, 3 miles off.

Still, it is a most pleasant 3 miles. The beach is smooth and exceptionally clean. The few pebbles at the tide line glisten brightly as each wave washes over them, leaving the small stones polished and pretty. The sea glimmers in the sunshine, and waves roll in inexorably, breaking white on the sand, then hissing as they drain back. You may find yourself playing tag with the erratic breakers, like a sandpiper, as you try to stay dry. On stormier days you may want to retreat up the beach and watch the waves pound the shore in relentless fury.

Bring binoculars, because many birds ride the waves. Look for grebes, loons, mergansers, scoters, and scaup during the colder months. Terns often skim the waves in summer. During spring and fall migrations, numerous types of ducks and other waterfowl rest here, and at times the beach is alive with sandpipers, plovers, and other

Off-season may be the best time to walk Ninigret's Beach

shorebirds. Gulls, of course, frequent the beach in all seasons. And once in a while there are surprises; on a March walk here I was escorted by inquisitive seals.

On your left, throughout the 3 miles, is the dune ridge. Because it is so fragile—and so vital—many pines have been planted to help hold the sand, grasses, and bushes in place. There also are sections of storm fences installed for the same reason, and signs indicate where the dune is to be left untouched and where visitors can cross. Respect the signs; even a few crushed plants can escalate erosion.

As you near the breachway, the beach grows slightly narrower and steeper. The piled stones that flank the breachway offer, along with a good place to rest, excellent views of the channel and the opposite side. In warmer weather you may see boats cruising the channel to and from Ninigret Pond and campers parked on the far side, which is the western end of Charlestown Beach.

When you are ready to resume walking, you have a choice to make. You can simply return the way you came, along the beach—

and most walkers do—or you can follow the channel rocks a few yards to the sand road that runs the length of the dune. Even if you are not planning to walk that road, it is worth a detour to the dune to see the salt-meadow plants growing there. Seaside roses thrive in dense thickets, decorating the area with purple and white flowers in summer and big orange rose hips in fall. The low-lying, pale green plants called dusty miller are easy to find, too, as are bayberries, vining beach peas, and the tall reeds called phragmites.

I've walked the sand road back a couple of times, and while there are attractions such as flocks of songbirds and more beach plants, the going is extremely tedious in the soft sand, and there are few good views of the pond until you are more than halfway back to the parking lot. Egrets, herons, and a variety of sandpipers and shorebirds do use the shallow pond, and geese and swans are invariably resting on the quiet water, but there are simply not enough good viewing spots to make the tiring walk worthwhile.

Instead, I recommend enjoying the beach walk back to your start, then crossing the parking lot for a good look at the pond, and perhaps a walk along it. You are likely to see swallows swooping over the water and find bits of shells, particularly of horseshoe crabs, along the shore. If you go in warm weather, also expect to see people wading in the water, searching for the abundant quahogs and littlenecks. You may want to try some clamming yourself, but even if you're not interested in the clams, the idea of letting that water cool your feet after 6 miles of walking in sand can be almost irresistible.

Napatree Point

Three miles of sand and seabird life, and a glimpse of military history

Hiking distance: 3 miles
Hiking time: 1½–2 hours
Difficulty: Easy; open beach on one side,
cove shoreline on the other

Save this walk for autumn or winter, when the swimmers and sunbathers have gone, the tourists have departed, and the boating activity around the nearby Watch Hill Yacht Club has diminished. Then Napatree Point is a great place to walk.

Napatree Beach is as far west as you can go in Rhode Island and farther south than any other mainland point. It reaches out into Little Narragansett Bay below Westerly like a slim, J-shaped finger.

All barrier beaches are fragile, and Napatree is one of the most fragile. Once it extended much farther into the sea, but the Hurricane of 1938 broke through it. The devastation was immense, with several lives lost and practically all the houses and cottages that then lined the beach destroyed. Now there are no buildings on the point, only the remains of a military fort, and the narrow strip of land is held in place against the forces of the sea only by its vegetation. For that reason, take extra care not to walk on or disturb the plants and bushes growing down the center of the point.

Napatree Point can be a good place for seeing birds, particularly migrating hawks in fall, but the birds that nest here require consideration from walkers. As a sign indicates, this is an osprey nesting area and there sometimes are sections of the beach roped off for the ground-nesting terns. Because of the birds, it is best to leave your dogs at home if you visit in summer.

To Westerly

Watch Hill
Yacht Club

Watch Hill Rd.

N

Little
Narragansett
Bay

Osprey
Pole

Cove

cabanas

shopping
mall

Osprey Poles

Atlantic
Ocean

Fort
Mansfield
Ruins

0   1/2
        mile

©1999 The Countryman Press

Access

To reach Napatree Point, take RI 1A to the village of Avondale, then follow Watch Hill Road until it reaches a little shopping center at the water's edge. You can see the yacht club on the right. Finding a parking place in summer is difficult, but at other times of the year, you should be able to park along the street or in the mall lot.

Walk through the shopping center parking area and follow a road that runs to the right, past private cabanas, to a fence barrier. There is room at the right end of the wire fence for you to enter the finger of land called Napatree.

Trail

You immediately have a choice. One trail runs along the cove shore at the right and another goes left over the ridge, between snow fences, toward the sea. For this walk, take the left path, even though walking in the soft sand is tedious. In a few moments you are facing the ocean and walking near the water, where the sand is firmer and less tiring.

Follow the beach to the right. This is the area most crowded in summer, but the entire beach is often deserted in winter, except for a few strollers and an occasional jogger. During September and October, you are likely to find a number of birders on the point, for Napatree is a key spot in the migratory flyway of hawks. When conditions are right, hundreds of hawks of half a dozen varieties will pass over the point in a single day. Migrating songbirds also pass this spot in both spring and fall, but many fly at night, so they are less visible.

Almost immediately, you can see ahead of you two high poles on the dune. They are topped by platforms, and at this writing one has an active osprey nest. Ospreys are the big, fish-eating hawks that once were nearly decimated by pesticides. Now they are recovering in numbers, and watching the graceful birds as they circle in the sky or dive after fish is a treat for Napatree walkers. Please do not disturb the birds or go too near their nests.

For more than a mile, you can walk a curving shoreline, gulls and other seabirds riding the waves on your left, starfish and bits of shells on the beach at your feet, and the low ridge with its beach peas, dusty millers, and other bushes and grasses on your right. The first two osprey poles are about halfway to the end of the point.

When you finally reach a jumble of large rocks in the water near the point's end, look for a narrow sand path uphill into a thicket of blackberry, bittersweet, and other bushes on the ridge. Hidden there is something most summertime visitors to Napatree know nothing about: the remains of Fort Mansfield. The fort was built around 1900 but almost immediately was found to be indefensible, and soon was abandoned and eventually dismantled. All that remains now are a few graffiti-marred low walls and concrete steps, a room or two, and the circular holes for the gun turrets, all hidden from shoreline view by the vines and bushes.

From the fort, however, you have a good view of the osprey nest poles (there is another on the J-shaped spit of land beyond the fort), and this also is an excellent place to watch the hawks in fall or to find the songbirds that dally here during migration. The rocky shoreline at the point often turns up sandpipers and other shorebirds, and there often are loons or cormorants just offshore.

From the fort, you can take paths down to the shore for the return walk along the harbor side. Look for a path that will take you across the narrow strip to the smooth cove that lies inside the curl of the J. (Walking the outside shore takes you to a dead end.) The cove is interesting because its shallow, calm water offers refuge for ducks and mergansers and also for the many clams, crabs, and other forms of marine life you may see as you walk along. The return walk also takes you much closer to the osprey poles than you were while walking the beach side. Footing on the cove shore isn't as smooth as on the sea side—more pebbles than sand—but it's still an easy walk back toward Watch Hill.

The harbor is a very busy place in summer, with boats of all sizes and descriptions coming and going or moored, and boating enthusiasts may want to linger here, just as birders often are reluctant to leave the point. By autumn, the boating activity declines dramatically, but there are usually some craft moored in the shallow harbor, except in winter, and the scene draws many photographers and artists.

The entire walk can be done in a couple of hours or even less, but if you like seascapes, migratory birds, boats, and invigorating salt air, it could, and should, take much longer.

Black Farm

A quiet, contemplative walk, with plenty to think about

Hiking distance: 2 miles
Hiking time: 1–1½ hours
*Difficulty: Fairly easy; mostly on open lanes, but
one narrow, shaky footbridge*

Black Farm, one of the state's newer management areas, is a place to come for slow, contemplative walking. Rather than spectacular, the 245-acre property is quietly beautiful, with lush groves of pines, lanes carpeted in pine needles, and an idyllic pond. You'll get good views of a river and walk a section of a long-abandoned railroad bed.

And there is more. On this walk you'll cross a hurrying brook in two places, check for wildlife in open fields, investigate a unique stone foundation, and pause at the grave of a Civil War casualty, a soldier who died at the age of 16.

As a management area, Black Farm is open to hunting, so it is best to hike in seasons other than late fall and early winter. Also, be aware that these trails are not blazed, so some care must be taken not to wander off onto other paths.

Access

Black Farm is in Hopkinton, on the Rockville-Alton Road. Take I-95 to exit 2 and go south. The parking lot is 1.5 miles on the left.

Trail

The parking lot is at the end of an open field, so before walking, take a moment to look over the field, which sometimes attracts birds and often features wildflowers. The trail begins at the far right corner of the parking area.

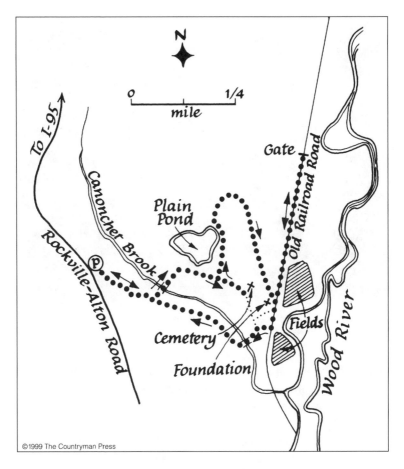

This first section is new and therefore not worn. There are some wet areas and a few places where roots or stumps from cut saplings can trip you up, so pay attention. You are walking through mixed woods with what appears to be a deep hollow on your left. In less than ¼ mile, the trail splits. Take the left fork; you'll return on the other path.

The left fork drops down a slope and crosses a quick little stream called Canonchet Brook. At present, only a makeshift foot-bridge exists, and crossing it might require some fortitude. Just to the

This unique foundation has both rectangular walls and rounded walls.

left of the bridge, a jumble of rocks shows traces of an old dam, once the site of a mill. Soon after crossing the bridge, you have to step across the narrow millrace from the vanished mill, then climb out of the little valley.

The narrow uphill path emerges onto an open woods lane near the pond. Turn right (going left leads you to a maze of trails, but won't get you to the features of this walk). In moments you reach an open area beside the pond, a good place to drink in the scenery. This is called a kettle pond, scoured out by glaciers thousands of years ago. It has no brooks running in or out of it. Surrounded by towering trees, it resembles a miniature northern mountain lake far more than its mundane name, Plain Pond, indicates.

Beyond the pond you reach an intersection. I recommend turning left—but not yet. First, continue straight ahead for another 100 yards or so, until you see a stone-walled cemetery on the left. This family graveyard includes the tombstone of Charles L. Collins, the teenaged Civil War soldier who died on the Mississippi River in 1863. His stone is inscribed with a touching poem. The Collins family once owned this land, and he is buried beside his parents.

When you are ready to resume walking, return up the lane to the intersection you passed earlier. (Continuing downhill from the graveyard would take you to the old railroad bed, but you would miss some good scenes of the pond and the forest.) This alternate lane, now on your right, takes you up close to the pond again, and then the trail curls through pines groves so quiet you can almost hear a needle drop.

When you emerge on the open roadway that once was a railroad track, look in the woods just to your right. There you will find a high stone structure that might have been a barn foundation or perhaps a holding pen. What makes it unusual is that some of the corners are the standard 90 degrees and others are rounded. I have never found any other stonework quite like this one.

Once you reach the old railroad bed, you have a choice. Going to the right would start you on the way back toward your car, but I suggest first turning left and following the straight lane, just to see more of the property. This segment resembles a tunnel, with the dense pines meeting above the lane. In about ⅓ mile you reach a gate across the lane. State property does continue beyond the gate for some distance, but several houses and dogs are close to the route in that area, so it might be prudent to turn around at the gate.

When you return to the area of the stone foundation, you are walking along a narrow open field, now on your left, and to the left of the field is the Wood River, perhaps Rhode Island's finest wildlife and canoeing river. In this area the river is wide and marshy, and often attracts ducks, geese, herons, and other birds.

Beyond the field, the former railroad bed runs through a thin strip of trees, then enters a larger open field where you may see hawks, songbirds, and, if you're very lucky, deer or a fox. At the far end of this field, you'll see a lane entering from the right. Take it. Immediately, you'll see still another junction. The trail to the right would take you back to the cemetery. Instead, take the left fork over a bridge. Unlike the rickety footbridge you crossed earlier, this is a wide auto bridge, and here Canonchet Brook is considerably larger than at the old mill site.

Just beyond the bridge, you reach another open field. At present, signs show this field as private property, but there is a strip of state land along the lower (to the right of the bridge) edge of the field. You can turn and follow a stone wall across this field, then return to woods through an opening in an adjoining stone wall.

This path also is new, and boot-catching small stumps lurk about. It runs through an attractive section of mixed woods accented by boulders. As you pass through openings at the meeting of two more stone walls, the trail forks. The more-worn path goes right, downhill, but that was once the lane down to the mill, and now it dwindles to almost no path at all. Instead, take the new, left fork. It carries you back to the parking lot in a few minutes.

Carolina South
A quiet walk for wildlife, solitude, and a glimpse of history

Hiking distance: 3¾–4 miles
Hiking time: 2–2½ hours
Difficulty: Easy; flat, open lanes and trails all the way

I f you like solitude—a place where you can walk for miles among the trees and brooks and fields without meeting other people—then Carolina South might be ideal. As long as you don't go during hunting season.

This is a walk through the southern section of the 2,350-acre Carolina Management Area in Richmond. I've changed my recommended route through this area since the earlier editions of this book, both to avoid backtracking and to take full advantage of the numerous little fields cultivated for wildlife. This walk, now 3¾ to 4 miles long, depending upon detours and exploration, will enable you to visit all the various habitats of the property and increase your chances of seeing deer, wild turkeys, woodcocks, and the numerous songbirds that make this such a delightful place in spring, summer, and early fall. The ambitious can easily lengthen their hikes by adding the Carolina North loop (Walk 9) or by simply exploring more of the south segment's fields.

There are other attractions, too, in addition to wildlife. At your start is a tiny graveyard, and much later you'll pass another cemetery, this one far back in the woods but surrounded by a white picket fence. There also are a couple of cellar holes along the trail, and you can linger at a small campsite for canoeists on the Pawcatuck River.

Be aware, however, that this area teems with hunters in late fall and early winter, and again for a brief period in spring when the wild turkeys are legal game. At most other times, Carolina South is left to the walkers and the wild creatures.

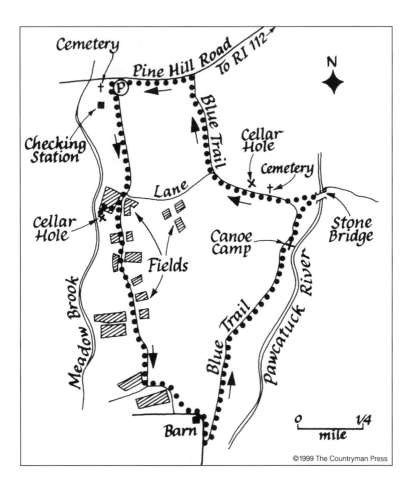

Access

To reach the starting point from the northern part of the state, take RI 138 east (exit 3 off I-95) to RI 112 just east of Hope Valley. Go south on RI 112, 2.5 miles to Pine Hill Road, turn west (right), and proceed for 1.5 miles. On the left is a red hunter checking station with a parking area in front. If you are coming from the coastal area on RI 112, go left onto Pine Hill Road just north of the village of Carolina.

Trail

From the parking area, first go a few steps and look over a tiny cemetery in front of the building, near the road. Dates on these stones indicate that the last burial was well over 100 years ago. This grassy little graveyard is a peaceful spot indeed, and sets the mood for this walk.

From the checking station, you can see the first of many fields planted in grain for wildlife. Take a minute for a look. Often small birds are in this field, and I've seen turkeys here. When you are ready to begin walking, take the lane that runs to the left from the building, going by an outhouse. This lane will be your main trail for the first 1⅓ miles of this walk.

The lane begins by running between tall pines, and you might feel you're on a forest walk, but within ½ mile you return to fields. Most are narrow strips; some lie right along the lane, others are carved out of woods and connected to the lane by short roadways. Don't rush by these fields; you never know when a deer or fox might be feeding right out in the open. Pheasants, quail, coyotes, rabbits, and hawks are other possibilities.

At the far end of the *first* field on your right, take a detour for another feature. A path going into the woods at the far corner of this field (see map) leads to a tumbledown cellar hole with a huge foundation for a center chimney. The path is narrow, and in summer the cellar might be difficult to find because of sprawling bushes. An even more obscure path continues beyond the cellar to more stonework of the vanished farm, and then to a rocky crossing over a stream called Meadow Brook. Exploring this area isn't easy, but it's fun.

Back on the main lane, you resume alternating between woods and fields. The lane itself often shows deer tracks, and in the right seasons you are likely to find many songbirds, butterflies, bees, and other interesting creatures as well.

When the lane reaches a T-intersection, go left. In a few yards, this lane turns to the right into a field. Now look to your left; across an open field you can see a dilapidated barn. Take a narrow path along the left edge of this large field (which is off state property), following the border of the field as it curves toward the barn. On your left will be trees and a low, damp area. Continue past the barn about 150 yards to a wide trail that enters the woods at blue blazes and a white sign—these show that this is part of the long North South Trail (Walk 40). You can follow the blue blazes for the rest of this walk, although my route includes a couple of short detours.

This trail, an old woods road, is the ultimate in solitude. Carpeted with pine needles, it can be walked in virtual silence. Less than ½ mile after entering this forest, and slightly more than 2 miles from your start, you'll reach an unmarked path going to the right. In summer, it can be easy to miss. This short path goes to the canoe camp on the banks of the Pawcatuck River. Years ago there were out-houses here and more-permanent cooking facilities; now it is just a clearing with enough room for a fire ring and a few small tents. Still, it is a good place to linger, look over the river, and perhaps have lunch.

Back on the trail, you'll see the first large boulders of this walk, along with some stone walls, before the old road forks. The blue blazes go left, uphill. I prefer going straight ahead, downhill, to an ancient stone bridge that crosses one of the brooks that feed the river. The property beyond the bridge is posted, so you'll have to turn back here, but the bridge, made of large blocks, is worth a look.

Returning to the blue trail is simply a matter of taking the first trail just up from the bridge. It quickly joins the main trail. Ahead now, on the right, is the second cemetery. This one, guarded by the picket fence, is not as old as the graveyard along Pine Hill Road; some stones are dated after 1900. The fence makes it unusual; most similar graveyards this far back in the woods are surrounded by stone walls.

Beyond the graveyard you'll find many stone walls and, just to the right of the trail, an extremely small cellar hole. On the left is a little clearing that formerly included several old apple and pear trees; now there are fewer each year. In time, only the stones will show that people once lived here.

Where the trail forks, you have a decision to make. The blue trail goes ahead (although the blazes are not visible at the junction, where they are needed most), and the left fork angles back to the

Easy, quiet walking is what brings some hikers to Carolina.

fields area you walked earlier. I usually have difficulty with this decision; the fields present more chances to see wildlife, but the blue trail is an idyllic stroll beneath towering pines. Consider it a win-win situation.

Staying on the blue trail adds perhaps ½ mile to your walk. You will reach a small parking area, then Pine Hill Road. Turn left, with the blue blazes, and in ⅓ mile you are back at your car.

Carolina North

Lots of laurel, pine, and hemlock; plenty of songbirds; and maybe a glimpse of a wild turkey

Hiking distance: 4 miles
Hiking time: 2 hours
Difficulty: Easy; virtually entire walk
is on open, flat lanes

S ave this walk for some bright morning in April or May. That's when a stroll through the northern segment of the Carolina Management Area in Richmond is most rewarding, because you will be likely to see numerous birds, possibly including wild turkeys.

Absent from Rhode Island for more than 150 years, wild turkeys have been reestablished through a state stocking program, and the big forests of Carolina are among their favorite habitats. Walking here offers other delights, too, but the turkeys make this place unique, especially in spring, when the gobblers are noisy. Be aware, of course, that Rhode Island now has a short hunting season for turkeys, usually in May.

This 4-mile walk is called Carolina North because it lies on the north side of Pine Hill Road, which slices through the 2,350-acre management area. Another ramble, called Carolina South (Walk 8), is on the opposite side of Pine Hill Road.

Carolina North's entire walk is on management roads, many of which are marked with name posts. Also, nearly all of this loop is blazed in blue, as part of the long North South Trail (Walk 40), so it is a very easy route to follow.

As with many management areas, dogs must be leashed if you walk here between April 1 and August 1, and fluorescent orange must be worn from mid-October to the end of February.

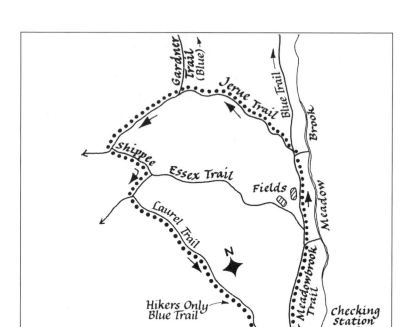

Access

To reach the starting point for both Carolina walks from the northern part of the state, take RI 138 east (exit 3 off I-95) to RI 112 just east of Hope Valley. Go south on RI 112 for 2.5 miles to Pine Hill Road, turn west (right), and proceed for 1.5 miles. On the left is a red hunter station with ample parking near the road. If you are coming from the coastal area on RI 112, turn left onto Pine Hill Road just north of the hamlet of Carolina.

Trail

From the checking station, walk Pine Hill Road a short distance west, following the blue blazes, and cross a stream called Meadow Brook.

At the first gravel lane going off to the right into the forest, you'll see signs indicating that a hikers-only trail is farther up Pine Hill Road, while horse riders and mountain bikers can use this lane. Even though you are walking, take the lane; you'll return on the hikers-only path.

This lane, called Meadowbrook Trail, is the chief access to Meadow Brook, a popular trout stream in spring. It is also heavily used in fall and winter by hunters, who scatter through the woods in search of deer, grouse, and rabbits. The lane is shaded by tall pines for the first ½ mile, and in May you are likely to hear numerous song-birds in the dense woods. There also may be turkeys gobbling and perhaps grouse "drumming," calling potential mates with loud sounds created by beating the air with their wings.

You will pass a barred lane that goes to the left. In this area are several small clearings and fields designed to attract and feed wildlife. The open lane ends with a cutoff to the stream. A trail continues ahead but is barred to cars and trucks. Just beyond the gate, the trail forks, with Meadowbrook Trail (and the blue blazes) going right and Jerue Trail, identified by a decaying sign, going left. Take Jerue; you'll find the blue markers again later.

Jerue winds around considerably more than the lane you just walked and is a bit more hilly. The forest is mostly second-growth hardwoods, with a great deal of mountain laurel in the understory. Dogwoods will be blooming in May, and there are numerous wild-flowers and ferns along the lane. When you reach a network of stone walls, indicating that this was once farmland, you are nearing a lane called Gardner Trail, going off to the right. At this point, you rejoin the blue trail, which turns and follows Gardner. The blue blazes will be with you the rest of the way.

Staying on Jerue, look for a venerable old beech tree leaning over the trail on the left. It's about ⅓ mile past Gardner. The tree is covered with carved initials and dates, some more than 50 years old and some very recent. Jerue ends at a T-intersection. Go left. This is Habrek Trail, although the signpost is gone. Forest is thick on both sides, with many young trees crowding the old road. You will be walking mostly downhill.

When the next junction is in sight, look on the right, in the

Some initials on this old beech tree date back 50 years.

forest, for the stone foundation of a vanished building. It is just before you reach a lane identified as Shippee Trail. If it's May, you'll notice in this area several old apple trees in blossom, an even more vibrant legacy to the vanished farmers than the foundation or stone walls.

At the junction, take another left. Going right on Shippee would take you to the Carolina Trout Pond. By going left, you are heading back into the interior of the forest. You'll see more old apple trees, more stonework, and many lordly pines. Now you are walking slightly uphill.

Shippee soon ends at a gravel road called Essex Trail. To the left, Essex would take you back to Meadowbrook. Instead, following the blue blazes, turn right onto Essex Trail; then, in about 1/10 mile, turn left onto a narrower path. State maps of the area call this Laurel Trail, and it's easy to see why. Mountain laurel is all around you.

You will follow this path for about 1 mile, all the way back to Pine Hill Road. It's a delightful section with attractive hemlocks, tunnels through young pines, and some open woods dotted with large boulders, in addition to the impressive thickets of laurel. The laurel may make you want to return in June, when it will be in bloom.

When you begin seeing stone walls, you are near Pine Hill Road. You will emerge, through the hikers-only fence, near utility pole No. 71. Turn left, round a bend, and you will quickly reach Meadowbrook Trail (at pole No. 68) where you entered the forest. Your car is just ahead on the right.

Long Pond–Ell Pond

10

Spectacular scenery from outcroppings above ponds, a "magnificent mile" of rhododendrons and hemlocks, and a glimpse of remnants of the past

Hiking distance: 5½ miles
Hiking time: 3–4 hours
Difficulty: Strenuous in the first and last mile with much rock climbing; easy in the middle segment

This walk in Hopkinton is through a rocky forest now called the Long Pond–Ell Pond Natural Area, and outstanding natural features are just what you will find. The first section is so spectacular that it might be called the magnificent mile.

In addition to Long Pond and Ell Pond, both of which you'll see from high above, you'll visit a bizarre network of stone walls and rock piles near picturesque Ashville Pond, then return via two roads and a retracing of the wonderful segment around Ell Pond and Long Pond. A full circuit is about 5½ miles and will take 3 hours or longer.

Keep in mind, however, that this is not a walk for the out-of-shape. Even though the high bluffs above the pond are barely ¼ mile from your start, you are likely to be huffing and puffing by the time you get there, and the climbs get tougher on the far side of the ponds. With two parking lots available, hikers concerned about the effort required can leave cars at each end of this first segment and do a one-way walk that would include all of the magnificent mile (but not the loop to Ashville Pond). The distance between the parking areas is about 1½ miles.

The yellow-blazed trail is the southern terminus of the Appalachian Mountain Club's (AMC) Narragansett Trail (Walk 11), which also runs into Connecticut. Included in the full circuit are the detours to overlooks above ponds, a descent through a rock cleft,

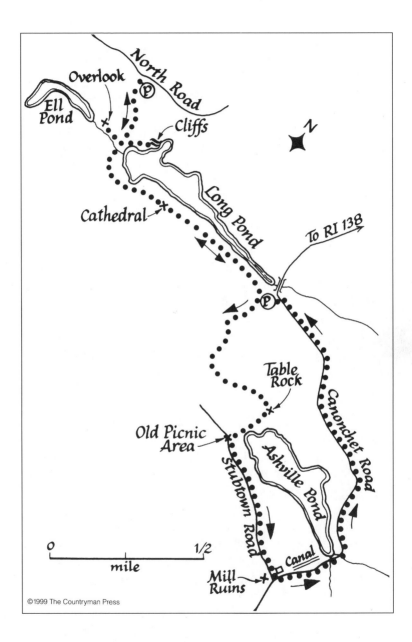

pauses beneath towering rhododendrons and hemlocks, a climb through a rocky, cathedral-like setting, and the "bonus" walk to Ashville Pond and back.

In 1974 this area—ownership of which is shared by the state, the Audubon Society of Rhode Island, and The Nature Conservancy —was entered in the Registry of Natural Landmarks because it "possesses exceptional value as an illustration of the nation's natural heritage and contributes to a better understanding of man's environment." A plaque with those words is embedded in a boulder above Ell Pond.

Access

To reach the start of this walk, follow RI 138 to the village of Rockville, near the Connecticut line, turn left onto Wincheck Pond Road, then left (south) onto Canonchet Road. Drive 0.5 mile to North Road (the first right) and follow North Road for 1 mile. After the first 0.5 mile, the roadway becomes gravel. Park on the left, where you see a sign and the yellow AMC trail blazes. There is another parking lot 0.5 mile south on Canonchet Road, but the North Road access is closer to the region's best sights.

Trail

Almost immediately, you will be scrambling up, down, and around boulders, but you are just as likely to be looking above your head as under your feet. Some of the tallest wild rhododendrons in the state shade the trail, as do hemlocks and mountain laurel. In early summer the profusion of blossoms in the first 200 yards creates a gardenlike atmosphere.

After struggling up a huge, angular rock mass, you will reach a sign pointing the way to Ell Pond (right), Long Pond (left), and a hemlock forest (straight ahead, down through the cleft). Explore the side trails; they are worth the time and effort. These side paths are not blazed but are easy to follow.

The Ell Pond path is short, ending atop an outcropping just 30 or 40 yards off the yellow trail, beside the Natural Landmark plaque. Spread out below is narrow, L-shaped Ell Pond, one of Rhode Island's

High outcrops offer great views of Long Pond.

few true bogs. Unfortunately, the view is not as expansive as in years past because of the maturing forest, but it's still a beautiful spot.

No trees obscure the views of Long Pond available by taking a side path off the opposite side of the yellow trail. It's a slightly longer walk, but you can climb to bulging cliffs that tower above the pond. This spot is so scenic that I often pause here both before and after the rest of the hike.

Back on the yellow trail, ease yourself down into the cleft. It is steep and narrow, but an AMC work crew a few years ago made the going easier by rearranging some of the rocks into something resembling a curving stairway. Solid walls of stone loom above you on both sides of the trail.

At the bottom of the cleft, the trail curls to the right and crosses a brook that links the two ponds. The trail then begins climbing again, going left up the side of a steep incline. For the next ½ mile or so, the trail weaves up and around immense boulders and rock masses. One steep slope is what I call the cathedral; dense hemlocks form the ceiling, keeping the "room" permanently dimmed, and huge stones represent the pews. Pick your way up the narrow aisles until you reach the top of the slope. As you pass through here, you may find yourself speaking in hushed, reverent tones. I often do.

There is more up-and-down going beyond the cathedral, until you see a tumbledown stone wall. Now you are nearing the end of the magnificent mile. The trail follows the old wall for several hundred yards atop a stony ridge that provides views of the narrowing pond below and a few houses on the opposite shore. When you finally turn to the right, away from the pond, you will be near a short side trail (to the left) that runs to the Canonchet Road parking lot.

At this junction, the yellow blazes make an abrupt turn to the right, returning to forest in a thicket of mountain laurel. There are some other paths here; be sure to look for the yellow plastic rectangles. It is slightly more than 1 mile from the Canonchet Road parking lot to Ashville Pond. It's a far easier walk than the first segment, but nearly as interesting in another manner. You're likely to see more wildlife and tracks here, and after leaving the laurel thickets for a more open forest of hardwoods, you'll see the numerous stone walls and rock piles. The walls seem to have been built randomly, running at many angles and in all directions, and the piles similarly defy explanation. They might have been an effort to make more land available for plowing, but there are so many rocks still scattered about that this would have been an all-but-hopeless cause.

When the trail reaches an immense table rock, you are near Ashville Pond. Here the trail turns right, then curls down to the water's edge, and soon runs into an old picnic area beside the lovely pond. A shelter and some dilapidated outhouses remain. The trail officially ends at the picnic grounds' entrance on the nearby road, called Stubtown Road.

To return to the starting point, I prefer walking Stubtown Road to the left about ⅓ mile to Canonchet Road. At this corner, you'll see the remains of a mill across from a house that a plaque says was built in 1762. As you take Canonchet Road to the left, you'll follow a canal that was built to carry water from Ashville Pond to the mill. The road is built on what was the pond's dam, and on the opposite side of the road you can see the stonework that channeled a brook into the pond.

For the 1 mile from Stubtown Road to the parking lot on Canonchet Road, you walk between two forests. This is not a heavily traveled road, and walking it can be thoroughly enjoyable. On the way you'll pass, on your right, two lanes that run to an unseen state-owned lake called Blue Pond. A walk in that area is described in *More Walks and Rambles in Rhode Island* (Backcountry Publications).

When you reach the Canonchet Road parking lot, now on your left, you can pick up the yellow blazes once more. You'll be retracing your route over the ridges and cliffs of Long and Ell Ponds, but it's a chance to get another perspective of the magnificent mile.

Narragansett Trail

A chance to explore rock outcroppings and a spectacular ravine in a forest of mountain laurel, hemlock, and lively brooks

Hiking distance: 4½ miles
Hiking time: 2½–3 hours
Difficulty: Fairly strenuous; rocky footing, considerable climbing of outcroppings and crossing of brooks

This section of the Narragansett Trail is almost entirely in Connecticut, but because the loop begins and ends at the state line, and because it packs so many outstanding features into such a pleasant package, many Rhode Island hikers have adopted it as their own. Or at least they wish it was one of theirs.

Part of the Appalachian Mountain Club's network of trails, the Narragansett, after crossing the state line into Rhode Island, continues around Yawgoog Pond and then to the Long Pond–Ell Pond region. (For a description of that area, see Walk 10.) This walk also links with the long Tippecansett Trail, which runs all the way up to the Arcadia Management Area. So, if desired, walkers could begin here and continue north to the Hemlock Ledges Trail (Walk 13), Firetower Trail (Walk 14), Pachaug Trail (Walk 15), and even beyond.

However, for most of us, there is enough to explore and examine just in this loop to make a thoroughly enjoyable day hike. The distance can be as short as 4 miles or as long as 5½ miles, if a circuit of Green Falls Pond is included. Those who simply follow the blazed trail and take no detours, though, may miss some of the special treats along this walk, so I recommend going slowly and exploring some of the massive rock outcroppings just off the trail. There are many such ledges and ridges. Other features include the thickets of mountain laurel, several tumbling brooks, a lovely marsh (not on the trail itself), the remains of a spool mill, a log shelter, the picturesque Green Falls

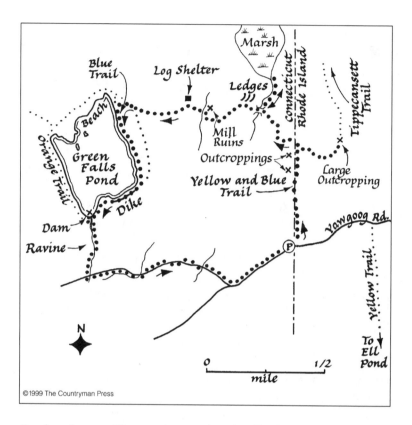

Pond, and a magnificent ravine. My listed walk of 4½ miles takes in all of these sights, along with a 1-mile return on a little-used gravel road.

This is a fairly strenuous walk, with considerable climbing up and down outcroppings. In spring and after heavy rains, you also may have to hop over some of the brooks. Of course, that is when the brooks are most appealing.

Access

To reach the start, take RI 138 west of the Hopkinton village of Rockville a short distance to Yawgoog Camp Road. Follow the paved road to the entrance to the Yawgoog Scout Camp, then turn right onto the gravel road that runs parallel to the front of the camp. Take the gravel road for 1.2 miles to the state line.

You will begin seeing yellow blazes along the road, but continue driving until the yellow trail goes into the woods on the right. At this point, you will also see blue blazes (the Connecticut trails are marked in blue). On the left side of the road is a concrete post that designates the state boundary. There is room enough for two or three cars to park on the right shoulder.

Trail

At the start, as you enter the woods on the right side of the road, you will be following both yellow and blue blazes, because this segment runs virtually on the state line. Immediately, you begin passing through the laurel thickets that remain green all year and blossom spectacularly in June.

You'll also quickly see the boulders, ledges, and outcroppings. Rocks are everywhere. With the right side of the trail posted, take some time looking over the ledges on your left. Short side paths lead to some intriguing formations. In about ½ mile the trail forks, the blue blazes curving left and the yellow going right. For now, take the yellow path. It drops through a small ravine, then climbs one of the larger stone ridges. This outcropping is considered the southern terminus of the Tippecansett Trail. By continuing north on the Tippecansett, you could walk all the way to Beach Pond and then on to the many trails of the Arcadia Management Area. For this walk, however, turn around here, return to the blue blazes, and head into Connecticut.

The trail climbs over boulders and ridges and soon reaches one of the rushing little streams. This is a place for one of the detours. Instead of simply crossing on the plank bridge, take a few minutes and follow a path upstream (to the right) from the bridge. Quickly, you'll reach another immense outcropping with numerous crevices and cracks that almost demand exploration. Also, you may be amazed that the tiny brook—only a few feet wide at the bridge—here opens into a wide and lovely marsh. The giant rock provides a great place from which to look over the marsh, and even though it is still early in your walk, you may find yourself lingering here for quite some time.

When you are ready to resume walking, return to the little bridge and follow the blue blazes. This next segment is easier than the first, running through a flatter section of woods liberally sprinkled with laurel. When the going becomes rocky again, about ½ mile from the brook crossing, you are nearing another brook. Here, amid the boulders, are remnants of a mill where wooden spools and bobbins were once turned. With some inspection, you can find a long, stone-lined tunnel that formerly carried water from the brook, through the mill, and back to the brook. Below the mill site, the brook splashes through a lovely, and lively, little cascade.

Just beyond the stream, the trail breaks into a small clearing dominated by a three-sided log shelter used by overnight campers. In a few more minutes, the trail reaches a gravel lane. You have now walked approximately 2¼ miles and are near Green Falls Pond. You have three choices: Follow the lane left to a dike at the edge of the pond; take the blue path down to the water and then turn left; or circle the entire pond to the right, passing a beach and picnic area on the way.

The lane to the left is the shortest route, but not the prettiest. I suggest staying on the blue trail. It goes to the right on the lane for a short distance, then turns left and follows another rocky brook down toward the pond. Just before reaching the water, the trail divides again. An orange-blazed path goes to the right, and a sign indicates that a full loop of the pond would get you to the dam above the ravine in about 1¼ miles. If you have the time and energy, do it. The route includes more boulders and laurel—more of a good thing—in addition to visiting the picnic area and beach.

For this walk, go left on the blue trail. Despite the dense laurel thickets, the trail provides some good views of the large but shallow pond, its rocky islands, and its forested shores. You may see ducks or geese on the pond. I've seen loons here as well.

The trail emerges on the earthen dike that was built along the lower end of the pond. The lane you crossed earlier passes just below the dike, then curves into the forest and runs out to the gravel road you will walk later, but please *do not* take this shortcut. You would be cheating yourself out of the climax of this hike.

Instead, walk the length of the dike, then, at its far end, pick up the blue blazes again and follow them into a grove of hemlocks. The trail crosses a ridge and runs down to a stone-and-concrete dam with a wooden walkway. The blue trail remains on the near side, instead of going onto the dam, but before dropping into the ravine, go out onto the walkway. On your right will be the pond, lapping placidly. But under your feet the water is spilling into a 40-foot falls.

The falls are even more impressive from below. Return to the blue trail (where you first reached the dam) and take it into the ravine. For many hikers, this ravine or gorge is the highlight of the Narragansett Trail. It is extremely narrow in places, with jagged rock walls looming on both sides. The tall hemlocks keep the gorge in permanent shadow, casting everything—the rocks, logs, roots, lichens—in an eerie green.

But don't spend all your time looking up. The trail is a bit tricky because it clings to the shore of the brook, and you have to negotiate numerous rocks and roots. As the gorge narrows and the brook goes into a series of drops, you even have to cross over to the right bank. When the water is low, this is a simple matter of stepping across the chute. When water is higher, you might have to find stepping-stones. Or jump.

Once on the right bank, the trail soon flattens, and in minutes you reach the gravel road. Here the blue blazes turn right. You, however, need to turn left. Your car is parked about 1 mile ahead. Normally, walking a mile on a road is an unattractive way to finish a hike, but because there are no houses and no utility wires along this road, and so little traffic, it's not hard to think of it as a wide woods path. There are plenty of stone walls, more brooks, and more hemlocks to enjoy.

Beaver River Preserve

A visit to a boulder-strewn forest and pristine river

Hiking distance: 3 miles
Hiking time: 2 hours
Difficulty: Fairly easy; rocky footing in places,
crosses river on narrow footbridge

This is a new place to hike, and well worth a look. A 214-acre sanctuary owned by The Nature Conservancy, the Beaver River Preserve in Richmond offers the walker a place to wander during hunting season, when roaming state management areas might be uncomfortable. There is much to see here.

The Beaver River itself is one prime attraction. Small but clean and picturesque, it flows between the two loops of the route described here. There also are several interesting boulder fields, some massive rock outcroppings, a bog that features sphagnum moss and insect-eating pitcher plants, the remains of a stone dam, and wildlife ranging from deer to butterflies. On my first visit here, I saw eight deer, six on the west side of the river and two on the east. Such sightings are not common, but at Beaver River you never know what you'll find.

Although there are two entrances to the preserve, it is easy to walk both sides of the river on one hike. I suggest going in from the west side, looping through that forest, then crossing the river, making another loop through the smaller area, and returning to the west side. The entire route is blazed except for a short segment on the east side, which I've included to make a loop.

The trail is attractive at any time of year, but when the leaves are down, you can better see the rocks and outcroppings that highlight this walk. And that also is when you might appreciate a sanctuary in which hunting is not permitted.

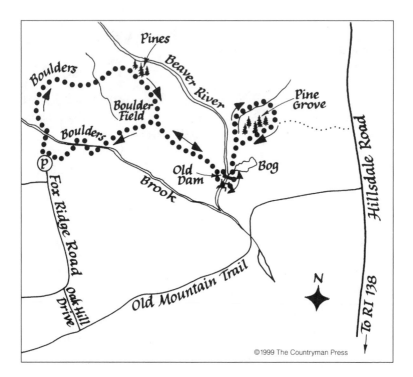

©1999 The Countryman Press

Access

From Route I-95, take RI 138 east just under 3 miles to Hillsdale Road, turn left, and follow Hillsdale for about 3 miles to Old Mountain Trail, on the left. Follow Old Mountain 1.1 miles to Oak Hill Drive, on the right. Take Oak Hill into a housing development. At 0.1 mile you reach Fox Ridge Road; take it to the right and continue until its end. At the end of this road is space to park; the trail begins straight ahead.

The second entrance to the preserve is on Hillsdale Road a short distance north of Old Mountain Trail, but the trailhead is obscure and there is little room for parking. Most of the best features of the sanctuary are on the west side anyway, so I strongly recommend using the Fox Ridge Road entrance.

Trail

Just a few yards from the parking area, over a low embankment, you'll see the yellow trail blazes. For this walk, take the left fork, doing the loop clockwise. Almost immediately, you'll see some of the boulders that dominate much of this section. The trail weaves among the large rocks as it climbs the small ridges and crosses seasonal brooks on plank walkways. Oaks are the most abundant tree, so if you go when leaves are down, you can see long distances through the woods.

As you circle through the woods, you drop to a lower area with smaller trees and soon find yourself walking just above a damp area of tangled undergrowth. Then, about ¾ mile from your start, you reach a pretty area of midsize pines. Beyond the small pine grove you can see, to your right, a slope covered with boulders of every size and shape.

The trail curves toward the boulder slope. Just before climbing the slope, however, the trail forks. You could continue up and over the ridge and soon be back at your car, with a walk of about 1½ miles. But you would be missing some of the preserve's best features. So I suggest taking the left fork and returning later to climb the slope.

The left fork, also blazed in yellow, is the connector between the west and east sections. It runs along what was apparently an old lane or cart path and, as such, enables you to easily pass through more boulder fields. On this stretch, some of the boulders are very large, several are split in intriguing fashion, and many are encrusted with lichens and moss. This connector, barely ⅓ mile long, is as pleasant to walk as any part of the main trails.

As you approach the river, you'll see a ridge, on both sides of the trail, that was part of a stone-and-earth dam built for a long-vanished mill. The trail runs parallel to the river briefly, then crosses it on an old, narrow footbridge. The bridge is your best spot for looking over the river, which at this point is a narrow, shallow trout stream. It becomes considerably larger downriver and eventually flows into the Pawcatuck River. You may see signs of otters along the river and, appropriately enough, occasionally a chewed branch that shows beavers use the river, too.

From the bridge, it appears the lane runs directly up to a house, but a few yards along this lane, the blazes turn left onto a side trail. This trail, narrow in places, runs a short distance to a bog where those interested in flora can search for the carnivorous pitcher plants that trap insects. Just before the bog, on the left, is a narrow, obscure path that leads to what is left of a stone dam. Here, when the river is running high, water cascades over rocks in a white, frothing fury.

The trail bypassing the bog is very low and sometimes flooded. If you have to turn around here, you will have a walk of approximately 2½ miles. When passable, the trail quickly goes, beyond the bog, onto higher ground in a grove of tall pines. As you enter the pines, look for an unmarked path on the right; this will be your return route from the eastern loop.

The yellow-blazed trail runs about ¾ mile from the bog up to Hillsdale Road, but I suggest making a ½-mile loop on this side of the bog and then returning to the connector. Upon leaving the pine grove, the trail passes a low stone wall, then enters a small clearing. Here, what appears to be a lane goes straight ahead; be sure to turn right with the yellow blazes. Less than 100 yards beyond this clearing, at another fork, the yellow trail goes to the left, over a small ridge. Instead of following it, go to the right on the unmarked path. This will take you on a short, pleasant loop back through the pines to the yellow trail above the bog. Then turn left and retrace your steps past the bog, over the river, and up the connector trail to the boulder slope.

After scrambling up the slope, you'll find that the final segment is much like your beginning: lots of winding around ridges, crossing plank bridges, and weaving your way through more boulders. And you might even see deer; this is where I found the herd of six.

Hemlock Ledges

Unique formations of glacial ledges, good pond overlooks, and massive hemlocks on the way to a "witness post" on the state border

Hiking distance: 3½ miles
Hiking time: 2 hours
Difficulty: Fairly strenuous in places; hilly and rocky

Hemlock Ledges is the middle segment of the long Tippecansett Trail through the Arcadia Management Area. At one end it links with the Firetower Trail (Walk 14), and at the other end it connects with the southern end of the Tippecansett Trail, which leads all the way to the Narragansett Trail (Walk 11). This section is short but sweet, adding sights not readily found anywhere else along the Tippecansett.

Both the hemlock trees and the glacial ledges and boulders for which this walk is known are unusually picturesque, and in this 3½-mile loop, you'll see unique formations of both rocks and trees. You will go as far as a witness post that marks the Connecticut border before returning to your starting point. It can be walked in less than 2 hours, but there are many interesting places where you may want to linger.

Access

To reach the start at Beach Pond in Exeter, follow RI 165 west about 7 miles from I-95. The pond, which extends over the state line into Connecticut, lies at the bottom of a steep hill. There is a large parking lot for swimmers on the right, beside the pond. There is also room for a few cars on the left side of the road, where this trail begins. A sign says that parking on this side is for FISHERMEN AND HIKERS ONLY.

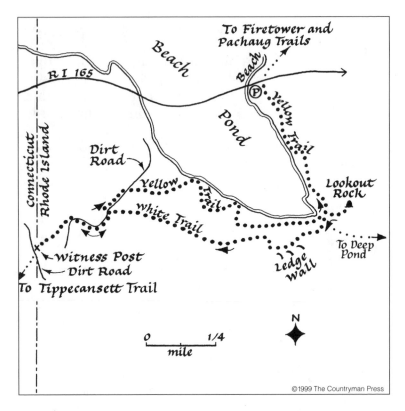

Trail

Begin under the sign TIPPECANSETT TRAIL on the left (south) side of the highway. On summer weekends, you are likely to find many anglers, walkers, and children in this area. The trail, blazed in yellow, runs just back from the busy shoreline at first and angles away from the water and several other, unmarked paths, thereby quickly leaving the crowds behind. The yellow trail goes into a thicket of mountain laurel and climbs a low ridge, then curves back toward the hemlocks and shoreline rocks. In a matter of minutes, you'll reach the first of the ledge overlooks at the very edge of the shallow pond, which in summer is decorated with blooming water lilies and an abundance of wildlife, particularly frogs, turtles, and birds.

The trail turns left with the shoreline, then leaves the water's

Many pond views are available along rocky Hemlock Ledges.

edge, and you can see a mass of jumbled boulders on a slope to your left. Here you'll also see numerous large hemlocks, and the canopy is so thick that the ground is permanently shaded. After a slight incline, the trail forks, with the yellow blazes making an abrupt turn right, downhill, and white blazes marking the path straight ahead, beneath a sign designating this route the Deep Pond Trail. Another white-marked segment goes left, beside a rock with LOOKOUT painted on it, up to an imposing rock wall. Take this detour first; it's worth a look.

In a few strides you will be at the base of a high outcropping. The path edges to the right and then claws its way up through a crevice. In minutes you will be standing atop the highest spot in the area. This roundish ledge enables you to see across the trees and Beach Pond to the woods and cottages on the Connecticut shore. For many hikers and climbers, this rock is their reason for walking Hemlock Ledges, and they often return the ¾ mile back to their cars after enjoying a visit here.

To continue the loop to the witness post, however, return to the junction and take the white-blazed Deep Pond Trail. The trail sign is nailed high in a tree just beyond the junction, and you will follow this trail only as far as the *second* DEEP POND TRAIL sign, also posted about 10 feet above the ground. It is important to find this second sign, because the path you want to take here is rather obscure and growing more faint each year. (You could walk to Deep Pond and back as an alternative to going to the witness post; see Walk 12, *More Walks and Rambles in Rhode Island*, Backcountry Publications.) Stay on the Deep Pond Trail for only about 100 yards; at a curve to the left, take a lesser-worn path that breaks off to the right. This route also is marked in white, but the blazes have become hard to find.

After 50 yards or so, the path reaches a vertical rock wall on the left, then follows the wall as it curves slightly to the left. Take some time here to inspect the trees—most of them hemlocks—that are growing out of cracks and crevices in the ancient ledges. Many are rather large, and they protrude from what appears to be solid rock.

Just as the wall dwindles in height, the path makes a right turn and crosses a seasonal brook. This is perhaps the trickiest part of the entire walk for following the trail, both because of poor marking and because dirt bikers have added side paths. After crossing the brook, which often dries up in summer, the trail goes left and then up a rocky ridge. From the ridge, an inviting path runs straight down, toward the pond, but that is a bikers path. Instead, look for the faint white blazes going to the left, into a thicket of laurel. This path will take you up and down several small ridges, then out of the hemlocks and into huge thickets of laurel. Time your walk for when the laurel is in bloom—usually early June—and this is a spectacular segment.

When you break out onto a dirt road, you have gone almost 1½ miles and have completed the most difficult part of the walk. You no longer have to worry about white blazes; they end at the road. Instead, you'll see the yellow blazes running along this road. Turn left and follow the blazes around a bend and then back into the woods, on your right. This forest is more open, with young oaks and blueberry bushes instead of laurel thickets. Within minutes you will reach a metal sign, the witness post. Less than ¼ mile from the end of the white trail, it stands beside a survey marker embedded in rock: the state boundary.

You could continue following the yellow blazes past the witness post all the way out to RI 138 and even beyond, to its merger with the Narragansett Trail. For the Hemlock Ledges walk, however, turn around here, retrace your steps to the dirt road, and follow the yellow blazes beyond the point where the white trail ended. The yellow trail reenters the woods, on the right side of the road, just a few yards beyond and downhill from the end of the white trail.

This route takes you through more dense laurel thickets as it winds its way back toward the pond. As you near the water, you will return to hemlock groves and large boulders. After visiting the water's edge briefly, the trail climbs a steep hill to the crossroads near Lookout Rock. From here, go left to return to your car.

Firetower Trail

A one-way, car-shuttle walk from
Beach Pond to scenic Stepstone Falls

Hiking distance: 4½ miles
Hiking time: 2–2½ hours
Difficulty: Fairly easy; mostly flat with brief segments
of up-and-down going and some rocky footing

This is an ideal walk for an autumn morning. It's good in other seasons, too, but when you pick a crisp day just after the leaves have turned color, you're in for a treat.

The Firetower Trail runs between two lovely spots, Beach Pond and Stepstone Falls. It is the northern end of the long Tippecansett Trail, maintained by the Appalachian Mountain Club, and is relatively short, just 4½ miles. Because making a loop that would include Stepstone Falls is difficult, this walk is among the few one-way hikes in this book. However, it can be linked with other trails (Hemlock Ledges, Walk 13, and Pachaug, Walk 15, at Beach Pond; and Ben Utter, Walk 19, at Stepstone Falls), so the ambitious and imaginative can easily extend the walk and devise their own routes. If you have only one vehicle and a 9-mile there-and-back walk seems too long, you can walk to the fire tower, then simply return to Beach Pond, making a walk of about 6½ miles and saving Stepstone Falls for another day and another walk.

This is not a walk to hurry through; take your time and enjoy the autumn forest. But do not plan this walk for late November or early December—prime hunting season. A section in the middle of this area belongs to a gun club and is actively hunted, particularly during deer season. So stay out at that period; there are plenty of other times to make this walk.

You will be in woods virtually all the way except for a short stretch on two public roads. The first segment is an easy stroll along

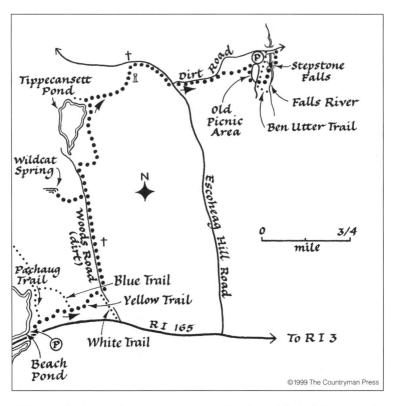

Tippecansett
Pond

Wildcat
Spring

Woods Road
(dirt)

Pachaug
Trail

Blue Trail

Yellow Trail

White Trail

Beach
Pond

Dirt Road

Stepstone
Falls

Falls River

Old
Picnic
Area

Ben Utter Trail

Escoheag Hill Road

N

0   mile   3/4

RI 165

To RI 3

©1999 The Countryman Press

old woods lanes, then there is a rocky but delightful area near
Tippecansett Pond, and you end with a downhill ramble through a
pine grove and an abandoned picnic area. Along the way, you pass
two old cemeteries, a wealth of stone walls, a spring, a pond, and the
fire tower for which this walk is named.

Access

For a one-way walk, you will need to place a car at Stepstone Falls.
Drive RI 165 west from RI 3 and I-95 about 5 miles to Escoheag Hill
Road. Turn right and proceed about 2.5 miles to a dirt road, Falls
River Road. You will see double yellow blazes on a utility pole at the
corner. Go right onto the dirt road and follow it downhill until you
reach a concrete bridge. There is room to park on the right. The falls

are just a few yards downstream.

To reach the trail's start, go back south on Escoheag Hill Road to RI 165, turn right, and drive about 2 miles to Beach Pond, which straddles the state line. You can usually park at the beach and pick up the trail at the spot where yellow blazes cross the highway. On the south side of the highway, the Tippecansett Trail is known as the Hemlock Ledges Trail.

Trail

At the start, the yellow blazes for the Firetower Trail run along with the blue marks of the Pachaug Trail for a short distance, going uphill from Beach Pond along to RI 165. Almost immediately, there is some steep up-and-down going, then the trail runs along the rear of an abandoned picnic ground now returning to forest and drops down a slope. As soon as you cross a dirt road, the paths divide, the narrow Pachaug going to the left and the Firetower Trail heading to the right on a wider lane.

Go right. It is time to enjoy the scenery. Maples, brilliant in autumn, glow overhead. Beeches, oaks, ashes, and young pines add colorful variety. The lane runs gradually uphill but is easy to walk. You will pass several side trails in this segment, including another blue-blazed connector to the Pachaug, but stay with the yellow blazes.

About 1 mile from the start, the trail turns left onto an open woods road that is maintained as a fire lane. White blazes go right; they eventually lead to Deep Pond (Walk 12, *More Walks and Rambles in Rhode Island,* Backcountry Publications). Stone walls run along both sides of the road in places, and many other walls can be seen in the forest. A short distance along this road you will pass, on your right, a family graveyard guarded by a splendid stone wall and an iron gate. Most of the headstones date from the 1800s.

The next landmarks, about ½ mile beyond the cemetery, are a sign and a white-blazed path, going left, that indicate a pleasant little detour to Wildcat Spring. The winding walk takes you downhill to a tiny spring that bubbles out of the ground beside a jumble of rocks and, at present, a fallen tree. The spring runs more freely in

The fire tower still looms above the trees along Firetower Trail.

April and May than in autumn, but is worth a look at any time. A visit to the spring and the walk back are included in the 4½ miles; skipping it will cut less than ½ mile from your hike.

Back on the yellow trail, you soon reach a sharp turn right, marked by double blazes. You are nearly to Tippecansett Pond and entering private property owned by the South County Rod & Gun Club. A sign bans ATVs and motorcycles but says hiking is allowed, provided laws regarding the wearing of orange during hunting season are followed.

The trail curves around the right side of the pond, but because of thick foliage, there are no unobscured views of the water from the trail. However, at the far end of the pond, where the trail turns away from the water, walkers can go a few yards on a lane for a good look at the pond. Along the way, you'll rock-hop across two brooks in quick succession. The second crossing is just below a dam made of rocks. The area is particularly inviting with beech trees adding, in fall, a golden glow over rocky terrain. There are several other lanes and paths running through this section, however, so pay close attention to the yellow blazes. In some cases, arrows nailed to trees will help you make the correct turns.

Where the trail makes a sharp right turn from an open lane into the woods, you should see, a short distance straight ahead, the shoreline of the pond and a gravel road belonging to the gun club. Walk to the pond; it's only a few yards. A feature at the present is a large beaver lodge standing in the shallow water.

Back on the yellow trail, you walk beneath more towering trees and beside stone walls. As you cross one of the walls, you'll see that you are leaving the gun club's property. Soon after, you'll cross a seasonal brook, then take an abrupt turn left. The trail then snakes its way up over small ledges and ridges. Then, suddenly, you emerge from the woods at the foot of the tall fire tower, which is fenced and locked.

Proceed past the tower to the paved road (Escoheag Hill Road). Take a moment to look over a well-kept cemetery directly across the road, then turn right and follow the pavement around a bend. Watch for the blazes on a pole beside the dirt road on the left. Take this road, Falls River Road, for the final leg of your walk.

You could follow the road all the way to your car, but after about ⅓ mile, the yellow blazes turn off into a pine grove on the right. Taking this path will lead you to the abandoned and all-but-forgotten Stepstone Falls Picnic Area, a favorite summertime playground of earlier generations. The trail emerges onto a crumbling paved road no longer accessible by car, then runs to the right toward a log pavilion. Here it meets the Ben Utter Trail.

You have a choice. You can take a yellow-blazed trail that runs to the left from the pavilion along a well-worn lane: It will take you to your car, just above the river. Or you can go a few yards past the pavilion on the Ben Utter Trail, then turn left onto a white-marked path. This is the one I recommend. The footing can be hazardous because it runs over hundreds of rocks, but this white trail will take you to the river, then along the shore to a footbridge just below the shelflike falls. You can cross the wooden bridge and follow a path on the opposite side to the concrete bridge and your car, or remain on the near side of the river. Either way, you will be able to finish your hike with great views of Stepstone Falls.

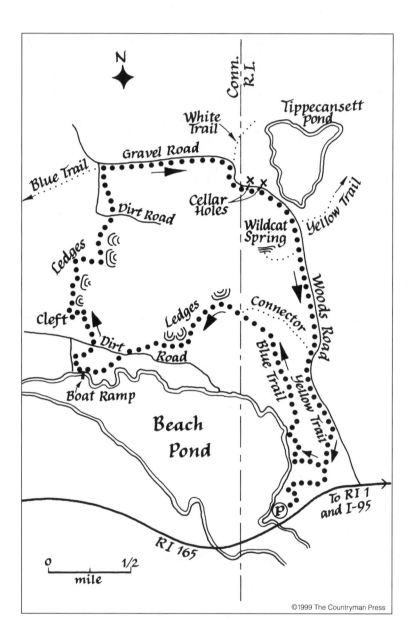

Pachaug Trail

A walk among glacial boulders and sheer cliffs through wild terrain virtually untouched since its formation

Hiking distance: 8 miles
Hiking time: 4–4½ hours
Difficulty: Strenuous with hills, rocky footing,
boulders in first half; second half is easy

Build up to this walk; try some of the shorter and easier trails first. The Pachaug will test your muscles and stamina. It's long—just over 8 miles—and the first 5 miles are among the most strenuous segments in this book. But it's a most enjoyable walk and a beautiful one. You climb over rugged ledges in the first part, scrambling up and down ravines and clefts, then finish with a few miles on flat old woods lanes.

This route is actually a combination of three hiking trails and runs a mile or more on an unmarked lane. You start in Rhode Island, swing around a pond into Connecticut, then return to Rhode Island past another pond and a spring.

Access

To start, take RI 165 about 7 miles west of RI 3 and I-95 to Beach Pond, which straddles the state line. You can park beside the pond either in the large lot on the right side of the highway or in the smaller lot on the left side. In summer, it's wise to arrive early, not only because the hiking is better at that time than in the heat of afternoon, but also because the parking areas can fill with swimmers, sunbathers, and anglers.

Trail

The Pachaug is blazed in blue, but you also will see yellow blazes for the long Tippecansett Trail. The paths run together upon leaving the Beach Pond parking lot, and you will be returning on the Tippecansett, which in this area is often called the Firetower Trail (Walk 14).

From the parking area, look for the blue and yellow blazes near the highway. The trail begins parallel to the pavement but within a few yards turns left and climbs a hill. This sets the tone for the first segment, which is very hilly and tends to loosen muscles for what lies ahead. In minutes, the trail levels off briefly as it runs at the rear of an abandoned picnic area, then it drops down a slope, crosses a gravel lane, and forks. The yellow trail goes to the right, your blue route goes left.

The blue Pachaug path curls back toward the pond, twice going down to the water's edge, before sweeping to the right through higher forest. You will quickly get a preview of the terrain ahead, for the trail is rocky and hilly. And it continues getting rockier and hillier.

If the going appears too difficult, you have an option. At a little more than 1 mile from the start, you will reach a registration mailbox at the junction of a trail coming in from the right. This path, also blazed in blue, is a connector trail to the yellow Firetower Trail, and you can switch to that route.

The cutoff is a short distance from the state line, which, if you remain on the main trail, you'll see marked by small disks nailed to trees and yellow stripes painted on trees. Throughout this area you are crossing brooks, skirting massive outcroppings, and walking beneath towering hemlocks. The ledges, many covered with mosses and lichens from permanent shade, are truly imposing, looming high above you. The trail runs at the base of many of these walls and occasionally clings partway up the rocks. The walking is not dangerous but requires care and attention, and therefore the going is likely to be slow. But places like this should not be hurried through anyway.

This rock-scrambling goes on for nearly 1 mile. Gradually you work your way down a slope and cross a dirt road. After another brief

Scrambling over rocks is a big part of doing the Pachaug Trail.

bit of up-and-down, you reach the pond's edge once more and then emerge on a boat landing. Here you leave Beach Pond behind for the last time. You are about halfway through the strenuous section, or roughly 2½ miles into the hike.

To continue, walk across the parking lot to the entrance road. At the point where the road enters the lot, the blue trail goes into the woods on the right. It climbs a ledge, then follows the edge of the parking lot before turning left (north). After crossing a dirt road, the trail levels off briefly. Don't be deceived; the most strenuous, but also most impressive, of the ledges are still ahead. Suddenly, the trail swings left and drops down a deep cleft that is, to me, the most spectacular spot in the entire 8 miles. Walls tower above the cleft on both sides, and it is steep enough that you'll probably have to use your hands in lowering yourself down. It's a great place to linger, perhaps while contemplating the might of the glaciers that helped create these formations.

From this cleft, the trail snakes back and forth along numerous other cliffs and ledges, nearly always running at the base of the high walls. This is wild terrain, virtually untouched since the glaciers; you have to go up and around, over and down the ledges, ravines, and boulders. The dense canopy of the hemlocks keeps the ground in permanent shade, and there is little underbrush. Tiny red squirrels are common and birds can be heard overhead, but the area has an eerie, intriguing aura found along few other hikes in this book. Being here is worth all the effort the hiking requires.

Eventually, the trail starts climbing and weaves its way out of the boulder-outcropping area, finally leaving the hemlocks and entering an area of laurel, hardwoods, and stone walls. You will cross a narrow woods road and then head slightly downhill through a very dense forest with thousands of young pines. In another ⅓ mile or so, you emerge on the next road, a gravel one. At this point, you have gone about 5 miles. The blue trail turns to the left, but for this walk, take the gravel road to the right. You should see white blazes along the road, for this is part of Connecticut's Canonicus Trail.

Your rock climbing and ledge viewing are finished. The rest of the walk is easy, but after the effort put forth, flat walking may be welcomed. As you round the second bend in the road, you'll see the white blazes and a path break off to the left. Ignore them and stay on the road, which by now is more dirt than gravel. Where the road makes a 90-degree turn left, a lesser lane goes straight ahead. *Be sure to turn with the main road;* the other lane will lead you astray.

Shortly after the road makes its left turn, you can find a large cellar hole just off the shoulder, on the left. In another ¼ mile, there is another old foundation on the left; this one is still shaded by lilacs and surrounded by periwinkles, flowers that in spring are a vibrant, living legacy to the vanished farmers.

In this segment you cross back into Rhode Island and soon you are walking along the western side of Tippecansett Pond. There are few views of the water, however, and the land on the left is posted as private property. Be patient; up ahead is a spot where the lane runs near the water and you can get a good view of the pond. You'll see some white blazes in this area and a few blue paint marks; ignore all of them and continue following the main road.

Shortly after passing the cutoff to the water, you will leave the pond behind and then notice the yellow blazes of the Tippecansett (Firetower) Trail. The blazes turn off this road into the forest on the left, but also run along the road ahead of you, which continues to be your route. For the remainder to this walk, you will be following the yellow blazes back toward Beach Pond.

In moments after rejoining the yellow trail, you will pass a white-marked path on the right. This is the route to Wildcat Spring. (For a description of the spring, see Walk 14.) A detour to the spring and back will add about ⅓ mile to your walk.

The rest of your walk is a reverse of the start of Walk 14. The yellow blazes take you along the woods road more than ½ mile, passing a tiny graveyard on the left; then the yellow trail turns right and follows a narrower lane. You'll pass a blue-blazed trail going to the right, which is the connector whose other end you passed at the mailbox several miles earlier. Eventually, the yellow trail takes you to the spot where the yellow and blue blazes originally split. From this spot, a left turn and a climb up the slope will take you to the old picnic grove. Beach Pond is just a short distance farther. After this walk, a refreshing dip in the cool water may be needed more than a picnic.

Escoheag Trail

A scenic descent through a rocky forest to a picturesque stream

Hiking distance: 3 miles
Hiking time: 2 hours
Difficulty: Fairly strenuous with rocky footing in
first half; easy on return route

The Escoheag Trail is a pleasant, scenic path on its own, but it can serve equally well as a warm-up for walks to other favorite Rhode Island hiking destinations. The 3-mile loop described here wanders downhill through a rocky forest, then returns along an unpaved woods road. Partway through the loop, the ambitious can make a detour to Mount Tom (Walk 20) and its panoramic views, and at this walk's far end hikers can easily extend the walk by going up to Penny Hill on the Breakheart Trail (Walk 18) or by following a stream to lovely Stepstone Falls on the Ben Utter Trail (Walk 19).

Features of Escoheag include an old picnic area with an imposing stone pavilion hidden in the woods, numerous little brooks that tumble through the woodland, and a couple of ledges that must be climbed and crossed. The same features that make this trail inviting, however, also make it a bit strenuous in the early going.

Access

To reach the start of Escoheag, take RI 165 west about 5½ miles from RI 3, turn right onto Escoheag Hill Road, and continue for 1 mile. Turn right onto a gravel lane next to a boarded-up log building. This is the old Beach Pond State Recreation Area, now used chiefly by bikers, horseback riders, hikers, and, in-season, hunters and anglers. Park in the lot to the right of the building.

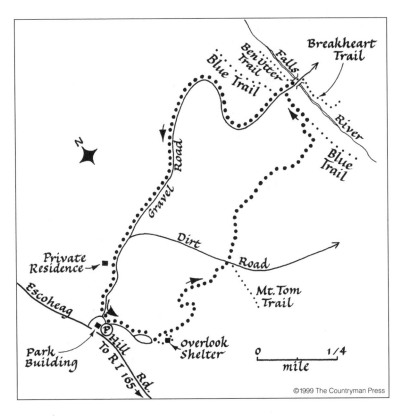

©1999 The Countryman Press

Trail

You'll see a small sign for the Escoheag Trail and white blazes going to the right along a gravel lane just beyond the parking area. This lane runs to what was a picnic grounds, and a few buildings and fireplaces still remain. At the end of this lane, the white blazes run off to the left, into the forest, and begin dropping down between boulders.

In moments, though, you'll notice a building above you on the right, perched on a high outcropping. This is the stone-sided shelter left over from the days when this was a popular weekend spot known as the Ledges Picnic Area. Side trails run up to the pavilion, and it is worth the climb. In winter and after leaves have dropped in fall, it provides an excellent view of the surrounding woodland.

When you are ready to resume your hike, climb down the ledge, but be sure to find, among all the unmarked paths, the white-blazed Escoheag Trail. It goes to the left, almost directly away from the ledge on which the shelter stands. You'll be passing through oak and beech groves, walking through laurel thickets, and climbing up and over rocky ledges. In spring and rainy periods, there are several little brooks that must be crossed, but all can be managed easily because of the numerous stepping-stones.

After topping the second major ridge, the going flattens considerably, and you'll notice PRIVATE PROPERTY signs just to the right of the trail. About 1 mile from your start, you'll emerge on a dirt road. Just to your right are white blazes and a sign for the Mount Tom Trail. Taking that trail, across Route 165, would lead you to some of the better cliffs in Rhode Island; a detour there and back to this spot would add about 3 miles to your walk.

The Escoheag Trail goes directly across the dirt road, known as Barber Trail, and runs mostly downhill for more than ½ mile. The footing is still rocky in places, but the walking is easy. When you start seeing pine trees, you are nearing an old lane that will take you out of this forest. On the overgrown lane, now growing narrow, you'll see blue blazes that indicate it is part of the long North South Trail, and a sign calls the segment to your right the Sand Hill Trail. You will go left, and in minutes reach another dirt road. This is the road you later will walk back to your car, to the left, but first go to the right. The river is just a few yards away.

This is the Falls River, one of the most attractive waterways in the state. Just before the bridge, on the left side of the road, is a sign indicating the start of the Ben Utter Trail, which leads to Stepstone Falls. (See Walk 19 for a description of this trail.) A walk to the falls and back would add about 3 miles to your hike. Across the bridge, on the right, is the start of the Breakheart Trail. If you take it up to Penny Hill and back, following the yellow blazes, you will walk an additional 1¼ miles or so.

Even if you take neither extension, a visit to the rushing stream is a pleasant diversion. It is a clear, noisy stream that features natural and man-made waterfalls that cater to trout and fishermen. The river is a scenic place to linger in all seasons.

As you start up the road back toward your car, you'll notice the blue North South blazes crossing to a woods road on the right. That lane leads to another abandoned picnic grounds and, eventually, to Stepstone Falls.

Stay on the main road, passing a barway that prohibits cars and trucks from coming here except during hunting and fishing seasons. You may meet horseback riders on this road at any time, and mountain bikers frequently ride here as well. The road is easy to walk, though the grade is quite steep where it makes a horseshoe bend to the right. Forest crowds in on both sides, and numerous seasonal brooks trickle underneath. On days when there is no other traffic, this road is as delightful to walk as a wilderness path.

You will pass a dirt road going to the left (this is Barber Trail, which you crossed earlier) and, in another ⅓ mile, a residence on the right and another gate that regulates traffic. Then it's just a few more steps to your car beside the old park building.

Frosty Hollow Trail

A long, winding walk in pine forests, through an abandoned camp complex to Penny Hill, then back along an enchanting brook

Hiking distance: 7¼ miles
Hiking time: 3½–4 hours
Difficulty: Long but easy except for a hilly section
in the middle and a rocky, often muddy segment
near the end

I f you like woods walking and are in no hurry to get anywhere in particular, Frosty Hollow is your trail. It wanders around in an erratic manner and ends where it began, but it can be a thoroughly enjoyable walk.

Still another walk in the Arcadia Management Area, this route is a combination of three established paths and incorporates a segment of road. It begins at a tiny trout pond, goes past a small campground, winds through a delightful pine forest, crosses a stream, visits an abandoned complex of cabins, then climbs up Penny Hill. That's only the first half of this walk. You then walk a mile down a quiet road, swing through woods on an obscure path, cross a parklike section, visit lovely Breakheart Pond and its fish ladder, then finish up by following an idyllic brook through thickets of mountain laurel.

This hike has lengthened slightly in recent years; a footbridge over Breakheart Brook has been removed, and the trail has changed in some other ways. Some sections are now more open and better blazed than previously, while others are perhaps more difficult to follow than before. However, there are several optional cutoffs that can be used to shorten distances and omit more difficult areas.

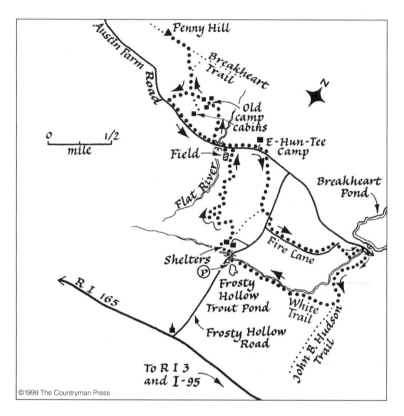

Access

To reach the starting point, take RI 165 west from RI 3 about 3 miles to Frosty Hollow Road, then turn right at the West Exeter Baptist Church. In less than 1 mile, you will reach Frosty Hollow Trout Pond on your right. Park in the small lot between the pond and a stream, and look for the white blazes at the bridge that crosses the stream.

Trail

Officially, most of this route is on a path called the Shelter Trail, but because this route overlaps and uses parts of the Breakheart Trail

(Walk 18) and the John B. Hudson Trail (Walk 21), many walkers have taken to using the more lyrical Frosty Hollow name of both the gravel entrance road and the trout pond.

Begin by crossing the road bridge, then follow the white rectangular plastic blazes left into the forest. Almost immediately, the path swings right and soon reaches the shelters for which the trail is named. You will pass through the little camping area quickly, then turn left onto a woods lane normally closed to vehicles. The lane is an easy, open path carpeted in pine needles. In spring you will find violets, lady's slippers, bluets, and buttercups in bloom, and you likely will be accompanied by numerous forest birds, particularly thrushes, wrens, and tanagers.

After this lane passes through an opening in a stone wall and starts curving downhill to the right, look for a sharp cutoff to the left. Here the trail is easier to follow than previously. Wider now and blazed in bright white plastic, it wanders back and forth for about 1 mile through a dense forest dominated by tall pines. This trail eventually leads past a barway to an open field. A line of pines runs down the middle of the field, and the path follows just to the right of the trees to a sandy road, known locally as Austin Farm Road.

Still following the white blazes, you turn left onto the road, cross a nearby bridge, then turn right back into the woods. Once again, you begin on an old lane that narrows to a footpath. After crossing a small brook on a wooden bridge, the path forks. Go left. You will climb a rather steep slope and emerge suddenly amid several small cabins, part of the long-abandoned Beach Pond Camps complex. Once a bustling little village in summer, it is now a place of silence. On a recent visit here, I saw a deer strolling through the yard, now being swallowed up by young pines. Take a few minutes to look over the buildings and a rusting water tower also being engulfed by the surging woodland, then follow the blazes down a gravel lane that leads away from the buildings.

The blazes turn right at a crossroad, but first take the left path for a look at about a dozen more cabins on another knoll. Back at the crossroad, decide if you want to climb to Penny Hill. The trail to it is steep in places and the hill itself no longer provides the expansive

Forest is gradually engulfing the old Beach Pond Camp complex.

views it once did, but most hikers feel the walk, less than 1 mile from this crossroad and back, is worth the effort. If you decide not to go that route, simply follow the gravel lane down to Austin Farm Road.

Those following the white blazes toward Penny Hill will find the trail forking, with white blazes going both ways. Take the narrower path to the left. (The right fork also goes to the Breakheart Trail, but would be used if you then wanted to go to the north end of the pond, not up Penny Hill.) The left fork runs through a rugged, boulder-strewn ravine, then breaks out onto the yellow-blazed Breakheart Trail. Now turn left, climb two steep slopes, and you will reach the rocky outcrops of Penny Hill. The summit, one of the highest points in the area, is about the halfway point in your hike and is an ideal place to rest. Thriving young oaks now blot out some of the panoramic views from the ledges, at least in summer, but this is still a special place.

To resume your walk, return down the yellow trail to the white trail (a sign again calls it the Shelter Trail) and retrace your route to the gravel road just below the old camp. Turn right and follow the camp road to Austin Farm Road. A left turn and a walk of about 1 mile on this road will take you beyond the stream and open field you passed earlier. Stay on Austin Farm Road until you reach the entrance to Camp E-Hun-Tee, a year-round youth home, on your left. Look to your right, directly across from the camp driveway, for an overgrown path with faded white paint blazes. It goes through a narrow gap in a stone wall into the woods. (If you are unable to find this path, or unwilling to try following the faint blazes, simply stay on Austin Farm Road to its junction with Frosty Hollow Road, then turn right.)

If you do enter the woods across from E-Hun-Tee, you'll immediately cross a motorcycle trail that runs parallel to Austin Farm Road. The going is tricky here; your path is not worn, nor are the blazes easy to see. But by looking carefully for the old white marks, you can follow this path as it wends through the forest, curling to the left. You'll cross two stone walls and another cycle trail in the ⅓ mile it takes to advance from Austin Farm Road to a tree with three small signs nailed to it. One arrow points the way back to the shelters, a second is for the trail you just walked, and a third indicates the route to Breakheart Pond South End. This is the path you want, but it is the least apparent. Still, there are more faded white blazes, and in moments you will cross a power-line path and then emerge onto Frosty Hollow Road. Just to your right, on the opposite side of the road, is a barred lane called Stone Trail. Take it.

You could walk Frosty Hollow Road back to your car—it's less than ½ mile—but then you would miss some of this hike's highlights. Stone Trail is an open, flat lane that runs through a parklike stand of tall pines and curves left before reaching a parking area for hunters coming in from Austin Farm Road. You could follow the driveway out to the road and then go right, to the bridge and to Breakheart Pond and its distinctive fish ladder. But it's better to walk along the right side of the parking lot and look for the old white-blazed path that runs down toward Breakheart Brook. This trail runs through a former picnic area—little remains now other than stone grill sites and an outhouse—to the brook. Previously, you could cross this rocky, picturesque brook on a footbridge, but it was removed recently because it had become unsafe, so now you must turn to the left and follow the brook the short distance to the road bridge. This gives you the extra treat of seeing the water tumbling over hundreds of rocks toward you; I think streams like this are much more attractive when followed upstream.

At the bridge, take a moment to look over the pond and the old, broken fish ladder once used to allow spawning fish to return to the pond. Then follow the opposite shore of the brook downstream. Here the path is the white portion of the John B. Hudson Trail, and the blazes are once more the rectangular plastic markers. The trail runs through a glorious thicket of mountain laurel, and seems to be climbing away from the water. Actually, it takes you atop a ridge that features steps down to the vanished footbridge and then a rocky (and sometimes muddy) section just above the gurgling, splashing brook.

Eventually, you leave the stream, climbing to the left up a steep slope, and then reach a junction with the yellow segment of the Hudson Trail. This is about ½ mile from the fish ladder. At this junction, look for a SHELTER TRAIL sign on a tree. Take this path, again blazed in white, to the right, and enjoy the final section of your walk. It gradually descends through a lovely area of laurel and pine back toward the stream. The trail will take you into the parking lot where your car awaits.

Breakheart Trail

18

Visits to Breakheart Pond and Penny Hill while crossing streams and wandering through pine and hardwood forests

Hiking distance: 6½ miles
Hiking time: 3–3½ hours
Difficulty: Fairly strenuous; flat and easy at the beginning and end, hilly and rocky in the long middle segment

Breakheart Pond and Penny Hill are picturesque places that have been popular with Rhode Island outdoorspeople for decades, but they are remote and not very well known to the general population. This 6½-mile route visits both places, combining an easy walk around the pond with a more strenuous hike through dense forest up to the hill's summit. The walk ends with a 2-mile-plus stroll along a little-used woods road. Don't let the idea of walking on a road dissuade you; many times walks along roads like this are very rewarding, particularly if you like wildlife. You will see more birds and mammals along rural roads than in dense forests, where the foliage is too thick and the walking too noisy.

This is another walk in the state-owned Arcadia Management Area in Exeter and West Greenwich. The yellow-blazed trail connects with the John B. Hudson Trail (Walk 21) at one end and the Ben Utter Trail (Walk 19) and Escoheag Trail (Walk 16) at the other, so extending your hike is easy. If you have a second car, you could leave it at Stepstone Falls and link the Breakheart and Utter Trails; your walk would still be about 6½ miles. Also, the Breakheart Trail connects at a couple of places with the Frosty Hollow Trail (Walk 17), and a detour on that trail to see cabins of a long-abandoned youth camp is possible.

In several ways, the Breakheart Trail has improved in recent years, particularly with the replacement of rickety bridges with solid new ones and the installation of bright plastic trail markers. However,

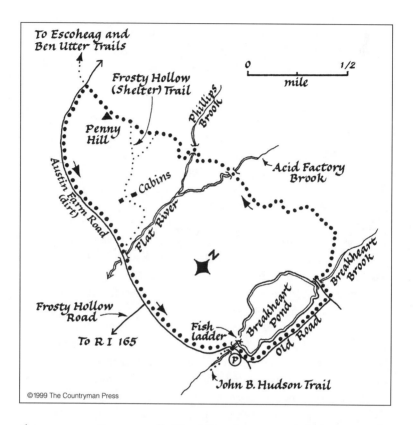

To Escoheag and
Ben Utter Trails

Frosty Hollow
(Shelter) Trail

Phillips Brook

Penny
Hill

Acid Factory
Brook

Austin Farm Road (dirt)

Cabins

Flat River

Breakheart Brook

N

Breakheart Pond

Old Road

Frosty Hollow
Road

Fish
ladder

To RI 165

P

John B. Hudson Trail

©1999 The Countryman Press

0   1/2
mile

there are negatives as well: Dirt bikers have carved their own paths through the area, which can make finding your route a bit confusing in places; and the view from atop Penny Hill is not quite what it used to be because of the growth of trees around the outcropping. Still, it's a walk worth taking. At the start of your route you can examine an old fish ladder and a small cellar hole, the pond and streams are lovely in all seasons, you'll pass through magnificent pine and beech groves, and perhaps you'll see several forms of wildlife, ranging from chipmunks and squirrels to grouse, deer, beavers, and wild turkeys.

Access

To reach Breakheart Pond, take RI 165 exactly 3 miles west of RI 3. Turn right (north) at the West Exeter Baptist Church onto gravel

Frosty Hollow Road, continue 1.5 miles to its end, then go right onto another gravel road until it ends at the pond. Cross the bridge over Breakheart Brook and park just beyond it.

Trail

Before starting your walk, look over the dam and concrete fish ladder beside the parking area. Consisting of a series of shallow, rectangular pools, the fish ladder was built to help trout get over the dam and return upstream to spawn. Although broken in places now and of little use to fish, it is one of the few such ladders remaining in the state. Also, go up onto the earthen dam for a look at the pond. Popular with anglers, it also draws waterfowl during migration periods and occasionally you may see an otter, beaver, or muskrat swimming about. The pond, as well as Breakheart Brook and Breakheart Road, derives its name from nearby Breakheart Hill, which got its name from the heartbreaking task of driving oxen and horses up its slopes long ago.

To follow the Breakheart Trail, take the old road from the parking area past a barway, then turn left onto a narrower lane that appears to circle the pond. At this corner, on the left, is the small cellar hole. There are numerous stone walls through this area as well, showing that this was once farmland. You'll cross the first of many brooks in this segment and walk beneath towering trees, mostly pines.

At the far end of the pond, you'll reach another junction; go left, crossing another bridge almost immediately. Often there is beaver sign in this area; on my last visit a beaver dam stretched across the stream just to the right of the bridge. You could follow this road all the way around the pond, making an easy 1½-mile stroll, but the yellow trail turns to the right, into the woods, just a few steps beyond the bridge.

The trail follows the brook briefly, then angles uphill through dense forest. There are plenty of rocks but the footing is not difficult. Pines and oaks are the dominant trees, and the numbers of squirrels and chipmunks in the area increase accordingly. Years ago, while walking this loop, my young son counted 22 chipmunks and 12 squirrels.

You will cross a couple of unmarked paths; ignore them. At about 1½ miles from your start, you'll emerge onto an old woods road; here the yellow-blazed trail turns left for a few steps, then goes back into the woods on the right. Now, as you begin heading downhill, you can see, through trees on the right, signs marking the boundary of the University of Rhode Island's research area, called the W. Alton Jones Campus. No trespassing is allowed in the research forest, but if you walk over close enough to read the signs, you'll notice a motorcycle path running along the boundary.

The trail weaves and wanders for a while, and you'll cross the cycle path, but following the yellow blazes isn't difficult. You come close to the URI property line at a plank bridge over a lovely stream with a most unflattering name, Acid Factory Brook. Here, be careful. *Immediately* after crossing this bridge, the yellow trail turns left. (A wider path goes straight ahead, up a hill; it is a cycle trail and would lead you astray.) The yellow trail is now blazed here better than in past years, and you should have no trouble staying on the proper route.

The trail follows the brook briefly, then curves right and begins climbing into a dense pine forest. Often described in the past as parklike because of the tall pines and lack of understory, this grove is now in transition, with thousands of young pines filling the forest floor and competing to replace the aging generation still standing above. At a Y-fork in this grove, the yellow trail goes left and quickly reaches another brook, this one crossed on a two-log bridge. This is about ½ mile from the plank bridge and roughly 3 miles from your start.

For the next ½ mile, the going is flat and easy, through mixed forest, but the toughest section is just ahead. So is a possible detour. Just as you start up a rocky slope, you'll see a white-blazed trail on the left and a sign saying SHELTER TRAIL. This is a segment of what I call the Frosty Hollow Trail, and a walk of less than ½ mile on this white trail would take you to the abandoned cabin complex described in Walk 17. If you continue on the yellow trail up the hill, you'll soon pass another Shelter Trail cutoff, then go up a couple of steep inclines and finally reach Penny Hill.

At 370 feet, Penny Hill is no mountain, but it is one of the highest points in Arcadia, and formerly it provided panoramic views of the surrounding area. Now those views are available only in winter; in other seasons, leaves of the surging oaks choke off most of the long vistas. Still, the bulging rock outcrops are a good place to linger. Just over 4 miles from your start, the summit is an ideal resting or lunching spot.

Going down the opposite slope is easy, and in a few minutes you will emerge on a gravel-dirt road, Austin Farm Road. The yellow trail crosses the road and goes on down to the Falls River, where it hooks up with the beginning of the Ben Utter Trail and the end of the Escoheag Trail. So if you have left a second car at the river or at Stepstone Falls (the other end of the Ben Utter Trail), stay with the yellow blazes.

If you are returning to Breakheart Pond, however, turn left onto Austin Farm Road and walk. It is just over 2 miles back to your car, but it is a very pleasant 2 miles with good footing and plenty of birds, and maybe deer, to see along the way.

There are some side roads going off Austin Farm Road, but stay on the main road. It gently curves left, crosses a river, where you'll see more white blazes that are part of the Frosty Hollow Trail, and passes Camp E-Hun-Tee, a private youth wilderness camp (out of sight on the left). There are no buildings along the entire 2 miles. Once you pass Frosty Hollow Road, which you drove on your way to the pond, it is about ½ mile to the finish.

Ben Utter Trail

A leisurely walk along a scenic river,
culminating at picturesque
Stepstone Falls

Hiking distance: 3½ miles
Hiking time: 2 hours
Difficulty: Relatively easy; some damp spots, some
rocky footing

The Ben Utter Trail is perfect for walkers who prefer to think of moving through the forest as a relaxing pastime and as a means of viewing the handiwork of both nature and humans rather than as an endurance test. This trail, named for one of the pioneers of the Rhode Island trail system, is short, relatively easy, and very accommodating. Wooden bridges span the brooks, and stone steps ease your way up and down some of the steeper slopes.

Following the aptly named Falls River upstream, this trail passes the remains of an old gristmill and a sawmill, leads through thickets of mountain laurel and dense growths of ferns, and culminates at Stepstone Falls, one of Rhode Island's most beautiful inland spots. It also provides a look at an abandoned picnic area that once was very popular but now is virtually forgotten. The trail runs between two dirt roads in the Exeter portion of the Arcadia Management Area and links with the Firetower Trail (Walk 14), the Escoheag Trail (Walk 16), and the Breakheart Trail (Walk 18), so your day can be easily extended if desired.

The route described here goes to Stepstone Falls, then loops up to the former picnic area and returns along the river. An alternative return, of approximately the same distance, is possible by following a woods lane.

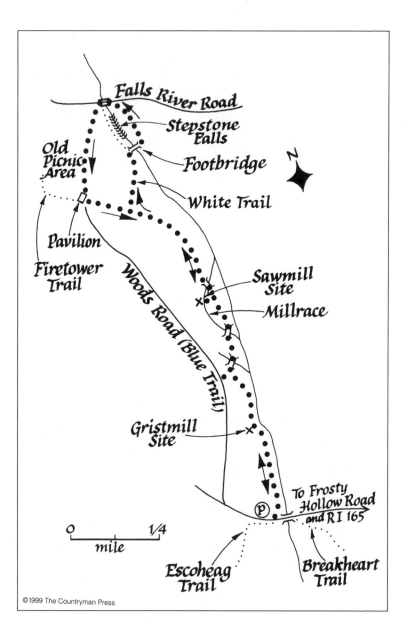

Falls River Road

Stepstone Falls

Footbridge

Old Picnic Area

White Trail

N

Pavilion

Firetower Trail

Woods Road (Blue Trail)

Sawmill Site

Millrace

Gristmill Site

To Frosty Hollow Road and R I 165

P

0   1/4
    mile

Escoheag Trail

Breakheart Trail

©1999 The Countryman Press

Access

To reach the start, take RI 165 west from RI 3 about 3 miles to Frosty Hollow Road. Look for the white West Exeter Baptist Church on the corner. Turn right onto the gravel road and drive to its end at a T-intersection. Go left about 2.25 miles until you cross a river. Park just beyond the bridge, on the right, where you will see a sign for the Ben Utter Trail.

Trail

The trail, blazed with yellow plastic rectangles, runs virtually on the riverbank at its start. You will immediately see and hear the first falls, although in this section they are man-made structures—huge logs anchored by rocks—installed years ago to make the stream more attractive to trout. The tumbling waters add a pleasing, soothing overtone to your walk.

After crossing a small brook on a wooden bridge, the trail goes left over a ridge that once was part of an earthen dam built for a gristmill. Stone steps lead both up the ridge and back down. Other stonework from the vanished mill is visible around the ridge and on the opposite side of the river.

As the trail passes a barway, you will momentarily break out onto a wider woods lane now used mostly by horseback riders. Blue blazes run along this lane, showing that it is part of the North South Trail, which stretches along Rhode Island's western border. You can walk this lane to the picnic area and then to Stepstone Falls, if you wish, but you would miss most of the river scenes.

Instead, stay on the yellow trail, swinging right immediately upon reaching the woods lane. Here you'll enter a thicket of mountain laurel, the shrub that in June covers the trail with pink and white blossoms. There is one short bridge in the thicket, and when you cross the next bridge (your third since the start), you are entering into a most interesting area. The brook under this bridge was dug as a millrace for a vertical sawmill powered by a waterwheel. Off the trail to the left you can see what remains of the mill, a rubble of huge stone slabs. Many of these stones have fallen into the water, but it is not

Stepstone Falls is beautiful in every season.

difficult to picture the effort that went into building the mill and digging the channel through the rocky ground. Another few yards takes you to still another bridge, again crossing the millrace, and off to the right you can see part of the dam that was built to divert water from the river to the mill. It's a good spot to linger.

Up to this point you are continually within earshot of the water, and the moods of the little river can make each walk here seem different. I've seen the river roaring over the falls in a frothy fury and I've seen it gurgling in a gentle lullaby. It all depends on the season, the water level, and the rainfall in previous days. Angry or serene, the many falls offer plenty of excuses for a pause.

Eventually, the path curves to the left, away from the river, and begins climbing. But just as you feel you're finally leaving the water behind, you'll reach a white-blazed trail breaking off to the right. Take this trail. If you remain on the yellow trail, you will go directly into the old picnic ground, but save that for later. For now, take the white trail back to the river.

The footing on the white path is very rocky, and there may be some muddy areas, but it's only about ¼ mile to a footbridge at the base of Stepstone Falls. This is another wonderful place to linger. The water sweeps in an idyllic manner over the flat, steplike stones that gave the place its name. Some of the falls are natural; others were created by a quarrying operation that took place here long ago.

Cross the footbridge and follow the white trail as it runs along the far side of the river, passing stone slabs that were cut out of the river but never used, and emerges onto a dirt road. Here, turn left, cross the road bridge, and return to the woods. You'll see blazes in both yellow and blue on a trail that angles uphill, away from the river.

Follow the blue and yellow trail; it will take you to an old log pavilion at the forgotten picnic area. A few other buildings remain, too, along with what is left of the paved road that once brought in dozens of picnickers on summer weekends.

At the pavilion, you'll see a sign for the Tippecansett Trail (this section is called the Firetower Trail in this book) going to the right, and blue blazes following a wider lane straight ahead. That lane will take you back to your start, joining the dirt road less than 100 yards from where you parked. The lane is pleasant enough, and certainly easier than following the river, but I invariably find myself choosing the yellow trail that runs downhill from the pavilion. That river is hard to resist.

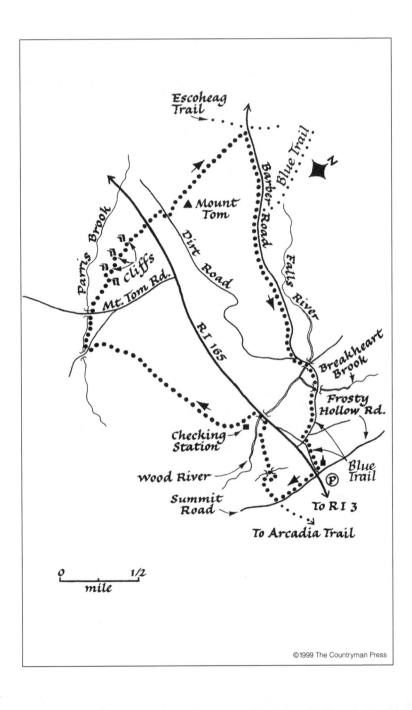

Escoheag
Trail

Blue Trail

Mount
Tom

Barber Road

Parris Brook

Cliffs

Dirt Road

Mt. Tom Rd.

Falls River

RI 165

Breakheart
Brook

Frosty
Hollow Rd.

Checking
Station

Blue
Trail

Wood River

To RI 3

Summit
Road

To Arcadia Trail

0   1/2
    mile

©1999 The Countryman Press

Mount Tom Trail

A roundabout route through a reforestation project to scenic Mount Tom's rocky cliffs and back along a dirt road

Hiking distance: 6½ miles
Hiking time: 3½ hours
Difficulty: Easy for long stretches, but fairly strenuous
on a rocky area in the middle of the hike

This wandering walk up and over Mount Tom in Exeter features a wide variety of attractions. Along the way you will stroll through a thriving reforestation project, cross rushing trout streams, and pause atop rocky cliffs with long panoramic views.

As a bonus, you can shorten your walk without retracing your steps, if so desired, by walking a highway back to your car. Complete this entire 6½-mile loop, however, and you will avoid the paved road, except for the few steps it takes to cross it twice and a few more to use a bridge. You will be returning along quiet dirt roads that offer excellent chances for seeing wildlife.

Spring is a great time to walk this trail. It's picturesque in fall, too, but you may run into numerous hunters then.

Access

The Mount Tom Trail, another of the many Appalachian Mountain Club (AMC) paths in the Arcadia Management Area, officially begins along RI 165 at a spot known as Appie Crossing, about 2.5 miles west of RI 3. This is the end of the Arcadia Trail (Walk 22) and virtually across the highway from the beginning of the John B. Hudson Trail (Walk 21). There is little parking space at Appie Crossing, however, and returning there would mean a walk along heavily used

RI 165 or retracing your route, so I recommend driving a few hundred yards farther west and parking near the West Exeter Baptist Church at the corner of Frosty Hollow Road. Look for a barred lane coming out of the forest near the front of the church; this will be your return route. Please take care not to park in the church lot itself, particularly if you arrive on Sunday morning.

Trail

To start your walk, cross RI 165 and go about ¼ mile down a gravel road called Summit Road, directly opposite Frosty Hollow Road. Ignore the first path into the woods (it is a motorcycle trail), and instead take the white-blazed hiking trail that crosses Summit at a slight bend in the road. Take this path to the right. (You could just as easily start by walking the dirt road in front of the church, but given a choice, I prefer using roads at the end of my walks, when I start feeling weary.)

In the woods, you go downhill at first, climb a hill, then weave through a low area and cross a small brook. Within minutes you'll find yourself walking through a pine forest, part of an area replanted years ago after 8,000 acres of timberland were destroyed in 1951 in one of the worst forest fires in Rhode Island history. Thousands of pines now thrive throughout this region, and all the scars from that tragic fire have vanished.

In less than 1 mile you reach the Wood River, a popular trout stream. Gravel lanes run along both shores for the fishermen. It would be shorter to wade through the stream and pick up the trail on the other side, but the white blazes lead you to the right over the RI 165 bridge and then back left on another lane and past a Quonset hut that is used as a checking station in hunting season.

Keep an eye on the blazes. The trail crosses a parking area near the river, then curves to the right and enters another pine grove. Here the path is wide, level, and easy to walk. The path is often flanked by wildflowers and in places there are huge anthills. You also are likely to find deer tracks in the sandy soil. (This area draws many hunters in fall and early winter.)

When the trail emerges onto a gravel lane, the white blazes go

High outcroppings provide panoramic views from the Mount Tom Trail.

left a short distance, then reenter the woods on the right near a small stream. This stream is Parris Brook and it is lovely, with numerous small waterfalls over man-made dams that were constructed to enhance the trout fishing. This segment is so pleasant that you may be sorry when it ends at a paved road, but the highlight of the hike—both figuratively and literally—is just ahead.

The trail crosses the road, Mount Tom Road, goes into the forest, and begins climbing. Once, a lane ran up this part of the slope, but now brush has virtually obliterated it. Still, if you look closely, you can find some stone embankments and walls that reveal the original route.

Within minutes you will be straddling a ridge. Cutoff paths lead to rock ledges, and the higher you climb, the more ledge you find and the better the views. From these overlooks, whether facing east or west, you can see for miles, and the scenery is all trees. It is hard to believe this is densely populated Rhode Island—it strongly resembles Vermont or New Hampshire. In early fall, the valley below is a patchwork of various reds, yellows, and greens. In spring, green of various shades dominates, with an occasional dogwood in blossom adding a dash of white.

The trail along the ridge is all rock. The adventurous and nimble can take shortcuts up and over the boulders. The less agile should follow the trail around the huge rocks. Both routes wind up at the same place—at the top of ledges that drop straight off. It would be a long fall, so watch your step. At the bottom of some cliffs rest great slabs of stone chopped off by glaciers. The high ledges are about halfway along this route, and a grand place to rest and enjoy the surroundings.

More up-and-down scrambling is ahead, but fewer open vistas, and shortly you begin descending to RI 165. The highway is roughly 3½ miles into your hike, and you can get back to your car by simply turning right and following the highway.

But Mount Tom itself still looms ahead. The trail crosses the highway and immediately starts upward. However, there are fewer rocks, no cliffs, and no overlooks on this part of the trail. For the most part, it is an easy but uneventful walk up and over the crest, which at 460 feet is one of the highest spots in the area. Unlike most hills, it is difficult to tell when you are at the summit.

After the initial climb, the trail crosses a lane (which could be taken, although it would cut off the wildlife road) and then runs straight and fairly level for nearly a mile. Bushes crowd in on both sides, and in places the trail is deeply rutted from years of use by hikers and bikers.

The trail ends on the dirt road called Barber Trail. Just to the left, the Escoheag Trail (Walk 16) crosses the road, and some hikers link the two walks. To return to your car, however, turn right and follow the open road. Closed to car and truck traffic except during trout and hunting seasons, the road runs about 2 miles, passing plenty of forest scenes and game management fields and crossing two streams that merge shortly below here to form the Wood River. In spring this is a delightful walk with a great deal of bird activity and numerous flowers growing on the shoulders of the old road. It is one of the better places for finding the tiny but fragrant trailing arbutus.

Near an old farmstead foundation, about ½ mile down this dirt road, you'll see blue blazes going off to the left; they signify the North South Trail (Walk 40). The blazes also run ahead along this road and you can follow them the rest of the way, although they are few and far between. After crossing the first bridge, bear right. After the second bridge, keep an eye on the blue marks. When they turn left up a gated lane, about ¼ mile beyond this second bridge, follow them. This lane takes you to the church and your car. If you miss the turnoff, you can simply stay on the dirt road until it reaches RI 165. Your car will be less than ⅓ mile to your left.

John B. Hudson Trail

A stroll through mountain laurel thickets and pine groves, a view of a fish ladder; a good introductory walk for children

Hiking distance: 3¼ miles
Hiking time: 2 hours
Difficulty: Easy except for a short segment along
Breakheart Brook

The John B. Hudson Trail, named for one of Rhode Island's hiking pioneers, is one of the oldest in the state trail system, and one of the shortest, yet it remains one of the most popular. It should be; it's a gem.

It is less than 1½ miles long each way, running from RI 165 to Breakheart Pond in the Arcadia Management Area in Exeter and back, but sections of it are downright dazzling, particularly in late spring, when the thickets of mountain laurel are in bloom, and in winter, when the gurgling stream that it follows for a while is as pretty as any picture with ice and snow. Two features formerly found on this trail, an observation tower and a footbridge, are gone. Both were dismantled when they became unsafe.

The trail, in addition to the natural beauty of the forest and the brook, still offers a look at a tiny cemetery and the cellar of a long-vanished house, and, at Breakheart Pond, a concrete fish ladder. All in all, it packs a lot of highlights into a round trip of about 3¼ miles.

Part of the region's vast Yellow-Dot Trail system maintained by the Appalachian Mountain Club, the Hudson begins almost directly across RI 165 from the end of the Arcadia Trail (Walk 22). At Breakheart Pond, it links with the Breakheart Trail (Walk 18). And along the way it crosses the newer, white-blazed Frosty Hollow Trail (Walk 17), so extending this walk on other paths is easy.

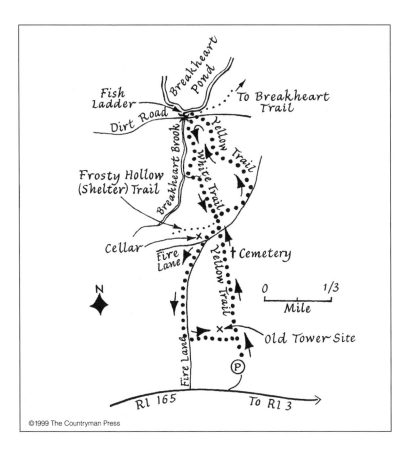

Fish Ladder
Dirt Road
Breakheart Pond
To Breakheart Trail
Yellow Trail
White Trail
Breakheart Brook
Frosty Hollow (Shelter) Trail
Cellar
Fire Lane
Cemetery
Yellow Trail
N
0   1/3
Mile
Old Tower Site
Fire Lane
P
Rt 165
To Rt 3

©1999 The Countryman Press

The trail loops as it nears Breakheart Pond, and a white-blazed option path allows you to begin your return by following picturesque Breakheart Brook. And rather than simply retracing your steps on the first segment, I suggest returning on a woods road that adds a pleasant area that includes the cellar hole.

This walk is a good one for giving small children a taste of hiking. Most of it is flat and easy, although the middle segment will involve some scrambling up and down steep slopes along the stream. That area is sometimes muddy and the footing can be treacherous, particularly in early spring, so if you're hiking with kids, wait until late May or June. Fortunately, that's when the laurel is in bloom.

Access

To reach the start, drive RI 165 for 2.6 miles west from RI 3. Check your odometer because the entrance lane, although marked by a small sign on a tree, is easily missed. The narrow, angling lane takes you to a parking area, on the right, that is veiled from the highway by trees.

Trail

Almost immediately after leaving the parking area, the trail forks. Go to the left, with the yellow blazes. You'll be heading slightly uphill into a grove of pines. At the *second* side path going off to the left, where young pines crowd the trail, you can detour to the site of the old observation tower that once provided a panoramic view of the area, until the surrounding trees outgrew the tower. The tower was recently dismantled, and at this writing only rubble remains. You will finish your walk by climbing this ridge from the opposite side.

Back on the yellow trail, you'll pass beneath towering pines and enter the first of many laurel thickets on this route. When the timing is right, this can be a stroll through a virtual tunnel of fragrant pink and white blossoms.

About ¾ mile from your start, shortly after crossing a low stone wall, you'll reach the little family graveyard. Although it is just to the right of the trail, and surrounded by stone walls, it is fairly easy to miss because of the surging laurel and pine. The few legible dates on the tombstones range from the 1830s to the 1850s.

Just beyond the cemetery, the trail crosses a fire lane known as Tripp Trail, which you will later walk in two directions. For now, take the yellow trail across the road. In a few yards, you reach an intersection. The yellow trail turns right, a white-blazed path also labeled the Hudson Trail goes directly ahead, and another white path called the Shelter Trail goes to the left. (The Shelter Trail is part of the hike I've called Frosty Hollow Trail in this book.) Take the yellow trail; you'll return on the white Hudson Trail. The yellow trail quickly emerges onto the wider woods road but follows it only briefly before cutting back into the pines. It then climbs a ridge and weaves its way downhill toward Breakheart Pond.

The trail leaves the forest at a parking area beside the pond. A bridge and the old fish ladder are just to your left. (For a description of the ladder and Breakheart Pond, see Walk 18.) This is a good spot for a break, but when you are ready to resume walking, look for a white-blazed trail running back along the near side of the brook, through a narrow fence opening and a sign that says HIKERS ONLY. This is a particularly lovely segment to walk. The trail alternately hugs the rocky, rushing stream and veers away through dense laurel thickets. At one point you'll find yourself at the top of a wooden stairway that formerly led to a footbridge. You could go down here for a close look at the brook, but there will be spots ahead where the trail itself is virtually on the banks.

Where the trail dips near the water, the going can be muddy and slippery, but the addition of many stepping-stones in recent years has greatly improved the situation. After about ½ mile of following the stream, the trail makes an abrupt left turn and climbs the slope, going up a seasonal brook, and then reaches the junction you passed earlier.

Here, you rejoin the yellow trail but follow it only the few yards to Tripp Trail, the open fire lane. Take this road to the right. It is easy to walk and delightful to look at, flanked by tumbling stone walls and overhanging trees. You will quickly see another road coming in from the right (that one goes out to Frosty Hollow Road), and in the corner where the fire lanes meet is the cellar hole. It is hidden in a tangle of bushes, including old forsythias that continue to bloom each spring.

Stay on the woods road for about ½ mile, until you reach the side path that takes you to the old tower site and back to your car. Finding this cutoff can be difficult, however. It is on the left at a point where the road makes a gentle curve to the right, just beyond an un-usually big pine on the right shoulder. The road widens a bit here and is flanked by young pines. At present, the path is marked with a small stone cairn, but cairns are not permanent. This path, if you can find it, will take you up a steep slope to the tower site. From there, it's a short walk back to the yellow trail and then ¼ mile to the right to your car.

If you happen to miss this cutoff, simply stay on the woods road to its end at RI 165; it's less than ¼ mile. Then turn left to reach your car.

Arcadia Trail

A one-way walk through rocky, sometimes spectacular, woodland

Hiking distance: 7 miles
Hiking time: 3½–4 hours
Difficulty: Fairly difficult in places because of
boulder fields and rocky brooks

The Arcadia Trail in Exeter has been rerouted often in recent years, so it's a must for veteran hikers who haven't been on it in some time. Now about 7 miles long, it includes such features as impressive stands of beech trees, rocky brooks, stone walls, quiet woods lanes, stone cairns, a mysterious chimney, great boulder fields, pine groves, and an idyllic fishing pond.

Unfortunately, this trail no longer goes through the Browning Mill Pond picnic area, a lovely spot in all seasons, but side trails do run there. Also, since Browning Mill Pond is roughly the halfway point in the hike, a car could be left there and the trail divided into two walks.

As before, the trail ends at RI 165, near the start of both the Mount Tom (Walk 20) and the John B. Hudson (Walk 21) Trails, so the ambitious can easily walk to their hearts' content.

I recommend making this walk in early spring because of the numerous seasonal brooks, which run highest at that time. These brooks, tumbling over thousands of rocks, are a delight in themselves, and in early spring they are usually decorated with marsh marigold, skunk cabbage, and other plants at a time when the rest of the forest is still winter-brown.

Access

As with other trails in the Arcadia Management Area, take RI 165 (Ten Rod Road) west from RI 3. If doing the full 7 miles, you need to leave a car at a small parking lot on the left side of RI 165, 2.5

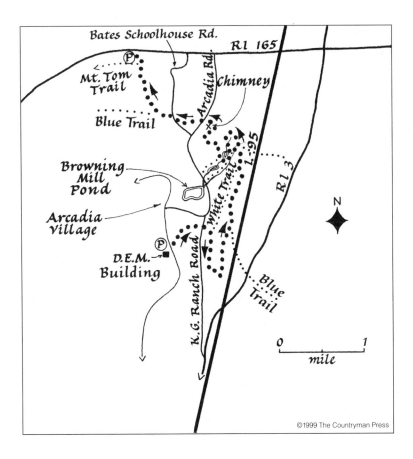

miles from RI 3. (The parking lot for the John B. Hudson Trail is almost directly across the road.) Then return 1 mile east to Arcadia Road and turn right (south).

You'll pass the Browning Mill Pond Recreation Area and can leave a car here if you wish to do the walk in halves.

To reach the official trailhead, follow Arcadia Road as it curves right and ends in the tiny village of Arcadia. Turn left onto Summit Road and drive another 0.5 mile to the state Department of Environmental Management complex. You can park in the visitors lot in front of the buildings. The yellow-blazed trail begins directly across the road.

Trail

You begin by walking through a grove of thriving pines, tall ones above and a new generation below. You'll also spot the first of the numerous stone walls you see along this route. In less than a mile, you reach and then cross a paved road, K.G. Ranch Road.

Shortly after reentering woods, the trail curves left. At the curve you can see, off to the right, granite slabs cut to hold something, possibly a granary. The woods here are more open than in the first section, with fewer young pines and more wet areas. At this writing, the Appalachian Mountain Club, which maintains the trail, is constructing bridges over some of the muddy sections and larger brooks, replacing those built in the 1970s.

Just after one damp segment, and immediately after passing through an opening in a stone wall, the path forks. The yellow trail makes an abrupt right turn. The more worn fork, going left, is marked in white. It is a shortcut path and links up with the yellow trail again, so you have a choice. However, you will miss quite a lot by taking the shortcut.

The yellow trail follows low ridges and wanders a long way through attractive, rocky woods. You'll cross the first of several boulder fields before jumping a stream and climbing over a stone wall slightly more than 1½ miles from your start. Here the trail makes a sharp left onto an old lane, then a right into a grove of red pines. This grove obviously was planted many years ago; the trees are lined up like soldiers in formation.

The detour into the pines is pleasant but brief. You soon return to the lane and then enter a clearing. Now you will notice blue blazes along with the yellow. The North South Trail (Walk 40) comes in from the right and joins the Arcadia Trail. You will have both yellow and blue blazes nearly all the rest of the way. In the little clearing, your trail turns left. But before proceeding, take a few minutes to look over a small cellar hole in this clearing, and just a few yards up the yellow-blue trail are a stone bridge and a small man-made pond, all reminders that this spot was once home to somebody.

For the next 1½ miles, the trail weaves through the forest, soon leaving the pines and wandering through a beech-dominated woodland. You cross several areas of boulders that might be difficult for short legs to handle, then cross more seasonal brooks. Along the way, if you are walking in spring, you should see many wildflowers, among them bluets, violets, wood anemones, spring beauties, and wild geraniums. This section is lovely in fall, too, with maples, oaks, and other trees joining the beeches in providing colorful foliage.

For a short distance, you are walking parallel to I-95, and you can hear the traffic, on your right, although only in winter can you see it. When the trail curves left, away from the highway, and enters a hilly area, you'll begin seeing cairns, stone mounds built on top of boulders. Who built them, and why? With thousands of rocks still scattered about, it doesn't seem that the cairns were an effort to clear the land. These mounds are not unique to this trail; they appear in several places in Rhode Island, but they give you something to think about as you walk.

In this area, about 3¼ miles into your hike, you are reunited with the shortcut white path, which joins you from the left. In another ½ mile you emerge onto a gravel road. If your goal is Browning Mill Pond, you can turn left onto this road and soon be finished with your walk of about 4 miles. You'll see blue blazes following this road.

The yellow trail, however, turns right onto the gravel road and runs into what was once a campground. Where the trail turns left into the woods, you can see white blazes and more blue marks going to the right. These blue marks are for the bicyclists and horseback riders who use the North South Trail, and lead to the abandoned Dawley State Park on RI 3, where the original Arcadia Trail began years ago.

Following the yellow blazes, you circle through a pleasant forest punctuated with boulders and brooks, a few of which you have to cross. Formerly, the trail swung through a wet area and followed the right shore of a pond. Now the trail goes back to the gravel road you crossed earlier, rejoins the blue blazes briefly, cuts off to the right through a parking area, and then reaches the pond. This pond, popular with anglers in spring, is scenic with nesting boxes for wood ducks and an old beaver lodge, currently unoccupied, on the far shore. The trail crosses an earthen dam and bridge, then returns to forest. A white-blazed path runs to the left, out to the highway and Browning Mill Pond on the opposite side of the road. If you want a closer look at the old beaver lodge, take the side path to the right, following the pond's shore. The lodge stands at the point where the shoreline turns left.

Back on the yellow trail, you enter a pine grove, then go through a section filled with briers, underbrush, and a complex of stone walls. The trail goes out nearly to the highway, then curves back inland. At one point, just after crossing a stone wall, you can see a large brick chimney in the woods on the left. The chimney does not appear to be from a house or cabin and there is often as much speculation among hikers about its origin as there is about the stone cairns passed earlier. Longtime residents of the area say the chimney was part of a bakery that once stood on the site.

The trail emerges onto Arcadia Road, crosses it, returns to the woods briefly, then breaks out onto a dirt road called Bates School-house Road. Back with the blue blazes again, you follow this road only briefly, too, for both sets of markings soon turn onto a barred fire lane identified by a decaying signpost as Bald Hill Trail. This ¼-mile stretch on the lane is one of my favorite segments of this trail. The lane is open and easy to walk, and birds and flowers are usually common here. The forest on both sides is hilly and rocky, and in spring dogwood blossoms add dazzling white decorations. Along this lane you'll also see a miniature stone-walled reservoir, one of the "water holes" built for fire protection in the 1930s.

Just beyond the water hole, the yellow trail leaves the lane, going to the right (blue blazes continue on the lane). Now you are on the final leg of the walk. This segment features low stone walls, boulders of every size and shape, and a fine mixture of trees. In just over ¾ mile after leaving the lane, as you drop into a low area, you'll see a white-blazed trail going left. This is the Mount Tom Trail, although not the part of that trail described in Walk 20. A short distance beyond this intersection, while walking between stone walls, you reach RI 165 and your car.

Wickaboxet

A stroll through a thriving young forest with a climactic view from an imposing rock ledge

Hiking distance: 6 miles
Hiking time: 3 hours
Difficulty: Easy; entire walk is on open, flat lanes, except
for a visit to a high rock outcropping near the end

Not many people visit the Wickaboxet Management Area. Those who do seem to cherish it. Many years ago Wickaboxet was a popular spot, but now it has been virtually forgotten. Yet it can be a marvelous place to walk, and it continues to get better.

Wickaboxet, a midsize management area at 679 acres, is in West Greenwich, just south of the Coventry line. It was the first state forest and once was extensively used for picnics and other outdoor recreation, but in recent years it has been overshadowed by the much larger Arcadia Management Area a few miles south.

These days, hunters use the place in autumn, horses are occasionally ridden along the old roads, and young people sometimes climb the area's featured attraction, Rattlesnake Ledge. But for the most part Wickaboxet, ever since a devastating fire in the 1950s, has been left to the grouse, squirrels, deer, and songbirds, and to the resurgent trees, which are again thriving and making the forest more attractive each year.

There are no marked hiking trails. Instead, you follow the woods roads. The 6-mile route described here runs along three sides of the state property, then returns to the interior for a stroll past rock ledges, and finishes with a climactic climb up Rattlesnake Ledge. No, you aren't likely to find any rattlesnakes; they've been gone for decades.

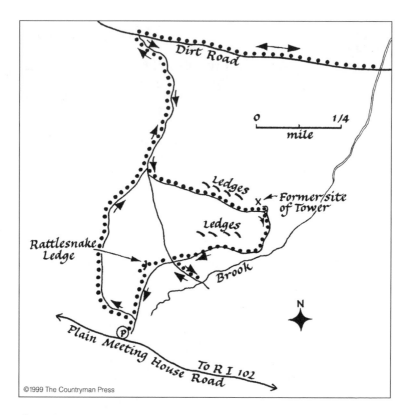

Access

To reach the entrance to Wickaboxet, take RI 102 in West Greenwich to Plain Meeting House Road, then drive west for 3 miles. A sign and a small parking area are on the right side of the road.

Trail

The entrance road is gated and forks almost immediately beyond the gate. Inside the fork, hidden in brush, is a small cellar hole.

Unless you are interested only in Rattlesnake Ledge, take the left fork. It is an easy, open lane that runs slightly uphill as it curves to the right. Immediately, you'll notice hundreds of young pine trees flanking the road. They were planted several years ago to hasten the reforestation that began decades earlier, after one of the worst forest fires in Rhode Island history. Now the young, vibrant pines complement the older hardwood trees; the mix of colors is particularly attractive in fall. Through much of this walk you'll see pines of various ages and sizes. Some were planted shortly after the fire, others were added much later, and some are natural offspring. The hardwoods, too, particularly the oaks, are doing well and are much more impressive than they were in the 1970s and '80s.

Birds abound. In the deeper woods, you are likely to see flycatchers, woodpeckers, chickadees, thrushes, and warblers. You also may see, depending somewhat on the season, waxwings, thrashers, towhees, and grosbeaks. There will be squirrels and chipmunks along the trail as well, and occasionally you may come upon a grouse dusting itself on the lane. Deer and foxes frequently use this road, so you can expect to see their tracks and/or scat.

Before you have gone 1 mile, your road will merge with one coming in from the right. You can turn here if you want a short walk; taking this loop back would make a hike of about 2⅓ miles. You would see some of Wickaboxet's features, including Rattlesnake Ledge, but would miss several miles of excellent forest scenery.

If you desire the longer walk, continue straight ahead at the junction, going north. Be aware that this route is a dead end; you'll have to come back. But I think it's worth the effort. The lane winds back and forth over low, sandy ridges, passing more dense groves of vigorous pines and oaks. At several points, stone walls will appear on the left, beginning and ending abruptly.

This road ends at a gate and an intersection with another woods road, shown on old maps as Welsh Hollow Road. Turn right onto Welsh Hollow Road, an inviting lane lined with tall trees and stone walls. (If you go left on this road, you quickly leave state property.) For nearly 1 mile, you can follow this road as it curves around boulders and crosses low hills. The farther you go, the bigger the boulders. Some, scattered through the forest, are immense. Also, you'll see numerous places where small rocks are piled atop boulders, most likely a long-ago attempt to clear some of this stony soil for farming. The

The view from Rattlesnake Ledge is of miles of forest.

road crosses a small brook on a stone bridge and soon after leaves state property. Metal posts mark the boundary.

A trail down this side of Wickaboxet back toward Rattlesnake Ledge would be ideal, but none exists. And bushwhacking is not advised because of swampy sections in the interior. So simply turn around and retrace your steps to the barway, then all the way back to the Y-intersection. Now take the left fork. In just a matter of yards, there is another fork; go left again. You will now be on a lane crowded with pines that threaten to engulf the path. Soon, though, the road opens a bit and you'll be able to see low rock ledges off to the left. At the end of a rocky ridge, you'll see a side trail that curls uphill to the left. Take it. It goes only a few yards to the top of the ridge, where a fire tower once stood. All that remain are a few concrete anchors.

After this brief detour, resume following the road as it swings downhill, running below another section of ledges, now almost obscured by pines. In about ⅓ mile from the tower site, you reach a crossroad. A detour on the narrow path going left takes you to a small brook that is lovely in spring. While walking this path once I was rewarded with the sight of a large deer that leaped up and bounded through the forest, flashing its white flag of a tail.

Back on the main road, just beyond the crossroad, begin looking into the woods on the right for Wickaboxet's famed Rattlesnake Ledge. Not far off the road, it looms high above the surroundings. It's a massive rock outcropping that demands inspection. Paths go around both ends up to the top. While you are not likely to find rattlesnakes, be careful anyway in climbing the ledge. A fall could be just as painful as a snakebite.

The view from the top is simply delightful, and surprising after walking more than 5 miles over relatively level terrain. You can see for miles over the treetops; in fact, your view is of what appears to be unbroken forest, possibly the longest such vista still available in Rhode Island. Take your time and enjoy the view.

When you are able to tear yourself away, take one of the paths back to the dirt road and turn right. It is only about ⅓ mile to your car.

Parker Woodland— Coventry

A walk with history: an old farm site and mill ruins, and a visit to mysterious stone cairns

Hiking distance: 4 miles
Hiking time: 2½–3 hours
Difficulty: Moderately strenuous; much rocky footing

A walk through Parker Woodland is a stroll through history. It enables you to take a look at the Rhode Island of 200 and 300 years ago in the stone remains of mills, farmhouses, roads, and fences. And it visits mysterious stone cairns that may be much more than three centuries old.

This trail is in the Coventry Tract of Parker Woodland, a large property owned by the Audubon Society of Rhode Island. (The refuge also spills over into Foster; see Walk 25.) The trail has changed some in recent years because Audubon now prefers that walkers start at a different parking lot than previously. The change makes the walk slightly longer but still includes all of the highlights of the area, including the scenic connector trail that allows the ambitious to lengthen the walk even more by including the Foster Tract Trail. This walk can be shortened at several points, but doing the entire route is recommended because each shortcut bypasses important features.

Years ago, the land now called the George B. Parker Woodland was considered a lively—and deadly—place. Two taverns that stood along Maple Valley Road, now the access route to the refuge, were known for the ruffians they attracted, and tales of shootings punctuate the region's history and lore. Local residents used to speak of troubled spirits roaming the older homes. Now Parker Woodland is extremely quiet, almost eerie, with its many reminders of the past silently reposing among the stately trees, surging undergrowth, and timeless boulders.

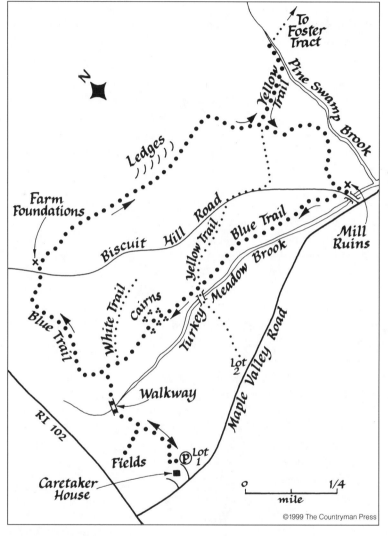

To
Foster
Tract

Yellow Trail

Pine Swamp Brook

Ledges

Farm
Foundations

×

Biscuit Hill Road

Yellow Trail

Blue Trail

Mill
Ruins

×

Meadow Brook

White Trail

Cairns

Turkey

Blue Trail

Lot
2

Maple Valley Road

Walkway

RI 102

Fields

℗ Lot
1

Caretaker
House

N

0   1/4
mile

©1999 The Countryman Press

Access

To reach the Coventry Tract, turn east from RI 102 onto Maple Valley Road. The first house on the left is the home of the refuge's caretaker. Just beyond is a large parking area labeled Lot No. 1. Begin your walk from this lot. Lot No. 2, where this walk formerly began, is about ⅓ mile farther down Maple Valley Road, and can still be used, but that lot is now open only on weekends in warm-weather months, and not at all in winter.

Trail

The trail begins behind a large kiosk that usually features Audubon Society news and wildlife information, as well as maps and pamphlets pertaining to Parker. The path, blazed here in orange, runs immediately into forest and soon follows the first of many stone walls you'll see on this walk.

At the first trail junction, the orange trail turns to the right, climbing over a stone wall on a wooden walkway. However, first take a few moments to walk to the left. This unblazed path quickly emerges at the edge of an open field, where you may see bluebirds or swallows using the birdhouses nailed to posts or hawks soaring above. It's a brief detour but often worth the extra steps.

Back on the orange trail, cross the stone wall and in moments you reach another raised walkway, this one a long, curving structure that enables you to cross a brook and swampy area. Go slowly; the water attracts much wildlife, from songbirds and frogs to salamanders and wildflowers.

Just beyond the walkway, the trail climbs onto higher, rockier ground and meets the blue loop trail. This junction is less than ½ mile from your start. You can go either way on the blue trail, of course, but for this walk, go left. The trail runs through a vibrant, mixed forest and the walking is fairly easy. On all sides, scattered through the woods, are boulders of many sizes, showing how difficult it must have been to farm this land.

Shortly after you start seeing more stone walls, the trail runs beside a low stone rectangle that was the foundation of a building, believed to be a barn, and in a few more steps you reach an old road flanked by stone walls. This is Biscuit Hill Road, a legendary passage supposedly named because a wagonload of biscuits meant for Rochambeau's army was spilled here during the American Revolution. You could shorten your walk by taking the old road to the right—it's an extremely attractive lane, and would take you down to

The mysterious cairns of Parker Woodland defy explanation.

a brook, the old mill site, and another crossing of the blue trail. But you would be missing some of the area's man-made and natural highlights, so instead, follow the blue trail directly across the road to the Vaughn farm site.

A sign beside a large cellar hole identifies this spot as the former home of Capt. Caleb Vaughn, and the sign also provides substantial background on the farm. This is another good place to linger, to examine the workmanship of the cellar and the stone-lined well, and perhaps to contemplate what life here may have been like so many years ago.

The trail continues through the "backyard" of the farmhouse, running through a grove of vigorous young pines, then through an extremely rocky area. You will work your way around and over ledges, some of which, lore has it, formerly were home to rattlesnakes and bobcats. For almost a mile after leaving the farm site, you weave up and down through this rocky area. You will cross one woods lane marked in white that provides another shortcut possibility, but you are better off staying with the blue blazes.

When you reach a yellow-blazed cross trail, beside an immense boulder, take a brief detour. The yellow trail, to the left, is the connector to the refuge's Foster Tract, but it is worth walking because it runs through a spectacular little ravine beside a brook. This is Pine Swamp Brook, and you will follow it upstream, advancing along a series of falls and pools while climbing down and past rugged ledges. Take the yellow trail as far as a bridge over the brook: still another great place to rest and marvel.

When you are ready to resume your walk, retrace the yellow trail back to the blue trail and turn left. (The yellow trail could be taken as another shortcut, but it misses the mill ruins.) The blue trail curls down near Pine Swamp Brook again, then up through the forest, and emerges once more onto Biscuit Hill Road. Just to your left, off the left side of the road, are the impressive stone remains of a sawmill and the stone-lined hole where the waterwheel stood. Also lying in the woods are the foundations of several other buildings that were part of the mill complex. Portions of what was a sluiceway can be seen on both sides of the road, and off to the right are a stream and a section of a dam that held the water for the mill. Now this stream, Turkey Meadow Brook, is a lively little current running over thousands of rocks.

There is more history, and much more mystery, still ahead. The blue trail follows Turkey Meadow Brook upstream, running along a ridge well above the water. In a short distance you will again reach the yellow shortcut trail at a bridge. The path across this bridge would take you to Parking Lot No. 2. Instead, remain on the blue trail, following the brook, and in a few minutes you'll reach what many people consider the most intriguing area of Parker Woodland, the stone cairns.

The cairns—cone-shaped mounds of stone—defy explanation. Archaeologists have studied many areas of Parker but they have not determined who built the dozens of cairns, or when, or why. Perhaps it is better this way; now each visitor can speculate on their origin. Were they built by Native Americans for some religious ritual? Did some pre-Columbian explorers use them to mark their way by the stars? Or were they simply the work of some fussy farmer who wasn't satisfied with throwing the rocks onto a pile?

Take time to look over the cairns and note their workmanship. Some have tumbled but others are filled with stones so meticulously fitted together that they are still solid after two or three centuries, or more. Restrict your study to looking, however; the Audubon Society forbids disturbing the cairns.

The cairns are a fitting climax to your visit to Parker. From the cairns, it is a short walk through a magnificent grove of beeches and another area of imposing boulders back to the orange trail (along the way, passing the white shortcut trail). All that remains, then, is a return across the boardwalks to your car, and much to think about.

Parker Woodland—
Foster

Farmland returned to forest revealing its
secrets in cellar holes, stone walls, and
a picturesque brook

Hiking distance: 4½ miles
Hiking time: 2½–3 hours
Difficulty: Fairly easy; some rocky footing, minor hills

The Foster Tract of Parker Woodland is not nearly as well known as the neighboring Coventry Tract (Walk 24), and is walked far less often, but it is a gem in its own right.

Officially named the Milton A. Gowdey Memorial Trail for the man who served as a volunteer caretaker for 30 years, this trail, running through a refuge of the Audubon Society of Rhode Island, loops through onetime farmland now returned to forest. You pass numerous stone walls, several cellar holes and foundations of vanished buildings, and a small stone quarry. On the 3-hour, 4½-mile route described here, you will also visit a picturesque brook that tumbles down a rocky ravine.

This trail can be walked in any season, but there are two special times. Come in autumn, when the trees are in their finest foliage and there are no worries about hunters (as can be the case on state management properties), or come in winter, when the brook is especially lovely with ice and snow formations. In winter, also, you have the benefit of animal tracks. Deer tracks, and sometimes the deer themselves, are commonly found here and once, while walking this trail, I saw a fisher—a relatively rare animal in Rhode Island—loping through the snow.

Be aware, however, that the parking lot recommended for this walk is not open in winter, so a visit then will require a longer hike, but one that is often worth the effort. Also, the parking lot is open only on weekends in the other three seasons.

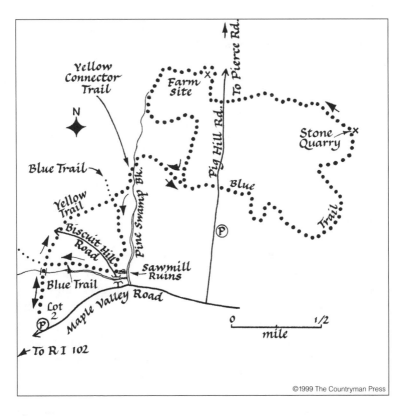

Access

The Foster Tract used to have its own starting point and parking lot, but that access was difficult because of deteriorating dirt roads, and the lot has now been closed because it was too hard to monitor. So it is best to start and end at the refuge's Parking Lot No. 2, about 0.5 mile off RI 102 on Maple Valley Road in Coventry. By starting at this lot, you'll hit some of the historical highlights of the area as well as use the yellow-blazed connector trail between the two tracts. One section of the connector is among the prettiest areas of the entire Parker Woodland.

If you want to walk only the Foster Tract, you can drive 0.3 mile beyond Parking Lot No. 2 on Maple Valley Road, turn left onto Pig Hill Road, and follow it until the pavement ends. A dirt road going into the woods will be crossed in just a few yards by the blue-blazed hiking trail. But starting at Parking Lot No. 2 is recommended; there is much more to see by beginning and ending your walk there.

Trail

If you start at Parking Lot No. 2, take a few minutes to look over the signs at an archaeological dig conducted at an old homesite by a Brown University team in 1983. The team also explored a charcoal-processing site farther down the trail. When you cross a rocky stream called Turkey Meadow Brook, lovely in every season, you have to make a choice. I suggest taking the yellow-blazed trail that runs straight ahead. You will return via the blue-blazed path that follows the brook.

The yellow trail is simply a connector between the two Parker tracts. It goes through high, rocky woods and in a matter of minutes descends onto an ancient road. This is Biscuit Hill Road, supposedly named for the spilling of a wagonload of biscuits during the Revolutionary War. The road is rocky enough that a hurrying wagon would be susceptible to disaster. The trail crosses the road and then intersects with the blue-blazed Coventry Tract Trail.

Look for a sign saying TO FOSTER TRACT beside an immense boulder, and follow the connector. (The yellow blazes are not always easy to see in autumn, when much of the underbrush is yellow and golden brown.) The path drops down to tumbling Pine Swamp Brook, which splashes down a ravine filled with jumbled boulders. It's an appealing area, particularly where the path goes right to the water's edge, enabling you to advance upstream. The brook is a series of falls and pools. When you see a low rock dam that creates a larger pool, it's time to cross the brook. There is a bridge, but in most seasons the brook above the pool is so narrow that you can step over on the boulders.

Still on the yellow trail, you soon leave the brook, climb uphill, and in a matter of minutes reach the intersection with the Foster Tract Trail, marked in blue. Turn right here, and you will quickly arrive at a narrow gravel road that is the abandoned portion of Pig Hill Road.

Cross the road, passing through an area of second-growth (or third- or fourth-growth) forest. The path turns often, and in this section you'll see a tumbled makeshift fireplace near the trail, another reminder that this forest was used by many people before it came into Audubon hands. There are at least two more of these fireplaces, most likely built by casual campers, farther ahead. About ½ mile from the point where you began the Foster walk, you'll see a rugged ledge on the left with several small caves at its foot, and you'll enter a pleasant, open section of woods as you skirt a small swamp.

Again, the trail is curvy and hilly. It's another ½ mile beyond the ledges before you reach the next feature. Off the trail, about 20 yards to the right, is an area of broken and piled stones left over from quarry operations. A closer look will reveal the foundation of a building. It is worth inspecting.

From here, the trail swings left around a slope decorated with large boulders and enters an area of taller trees. The walking alternates from descents through rocky lowlands to hilly but easy woodlands. Go slowly and enjoy the trees, mostly maple, oak, and beech. Soon you start seeing stone walls. After passing through an opening in the walls, look to the left. There is a fallen-in cellar hole there, but it is hard to see, especially when leaves are on the trees. Soon after reaching the stone walls, you'll pass a small, three-sided stone foundation and cross Pig Hill Road for the second time.

As you cross the road and reenter the forest, you'll see a map of the property nailed to a tree. This section is delightful, first for the tall pines, then for the network of stone walls that marked the fields of a vanished farm. Some of the walls remain high and straight; others are little more than tumbledown piles. When you reach a small cellar hole just off the path, pause and look it over. Somebody once lived here. Just beyond the cellar, a sign on a tree points the way to Table Rock. Take the yellow-blazed detour; it leads about 50 yards to a flat stone lying atop smaller rocks.

Back on the blue trail, there are many more rock structures to examine. The trail goes through a gateway in a stone wall, then curls around and runs parallel to the wall. When the path virtually touches the wall, look across it for an intriguing example of an ancient homesite. The cellar is much larger than the one near Table Rock, and nearly half of the cellar is taken up by the huge foundation of what

Parker Woodland is a place of quiet beauty these days.

was the fireplace and chimney. On the far side of the hole are the steps, and a tree is growing precisely where the long-ago farmers climbed into and out of the cellar. Out a few yards from the stairway, hidden beneath a large flat stone, is the family's well. Its circular, stone-lined walls are a work of art and invite inspection. But be very careful—old wells can be dangerous. And be sure to replace the stone over the hole.

From the farm site, the trail drops down a slope, curves left, and runs near Pine Swamp Brook again. Here it is not quite as lively, or as lovely, as it is along the yellow connector trail. The trail follows the brook only briefly, then curves left and climbs uphill, entering a pleasant, easy-to-walk section of forest. There are a couple of minor boulder fields, and a few stone walls that are bewildering. They wander at seemingly random angles, and few are connected. Most are just lines of rocks that simply end. Most likely, they were simply a means of clearing fields, but with all the rocks still evident on the forest floor, just how effective that clearing was is open to question.

When you reach a junction with the yellow connector trail, turn right and retrace your route along Pine Swamp Brook back to the Coventry Tract. When you reach the intersection with the Coventry blue trail, you have another choice to make. You can retrace your steps on the yellow trail all the way to Turkey Meadow Brook, but I recommend following the blue trail to the left. It will weave through a rocky area, then emerge onto Biscuit Hill Road. When you reach the old dirt road, take a few minutes and look over the remains of a mill site off to the left. (This site is described more fully in Walk 24.) From there, return to the blue trail for the up-and-down segment that follows Turkey Meadow Brook upstream. It will lead you back to the footbridge you crossed earlier, and the final short stretch to the parking lot.

Durfee Hill

A walk with the wildlife in the northwestern part of the state

Hiking distance: 3 miles
Hiking time: 2 hours
Difficulty: Fairly easy; some small hills

Formerly, people doing the Durfee Hill Trail walked all the way to Killingly Pond, which straddles the Rhode Island–Connecticut border, and back, a distance of 9 miles. But some of that trail ran on private property that has now been posted as off-limits, so your are advised to remain in the Durfee Hill Management Area.

The state-owned management area consists of more than 900 acres in Glocester, but it is somewhat disjointed, split by roads and sections of private property. The largest contiguous segment is a short distance south of the area chosen for this walk, but this loop was picked because it offers several of Durfee Hill's top attractions in terms of scenery, terrain, wildlife, and historical significance.

This walk is short—just 3 miles—but it includes a high, imposing rock wall that sometimes draws rock climbers; two lovely ponds; pine and hemlock groves; a marsh; open fields; a well-kept graveyard hidden in the forest; the stonework of a former gristmill; and enough up-and-down going to provide a workout.

In addition, there is always the possibility of seeing deer, beavers, red squirrels, wood ducks, herons, grouse, and many kinds of songbirds along this route.

Keep in mind, however, that no blazes mark these paths; some care must be taken to stay on the route outlined here and not to wander off onto side trails, many of which run off state land.

Also, remember that hunters know about the Durfee deer, and this area teems with hunters in November and December. Therefore, early autumn, late winter, and spring might be better times to explore

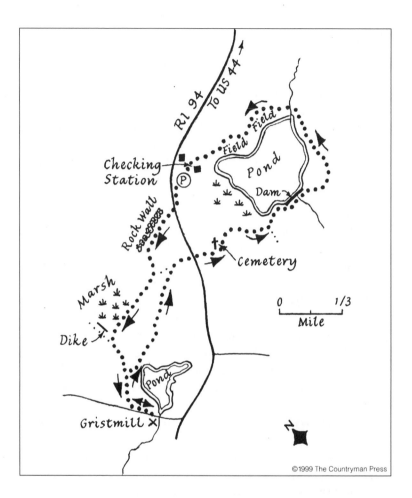

these trails. In summer, the dense conifers and ponds attract more mosquitoes than most hikers will want to fight.

Access

To reach the start, take US 44 in Glocester almost to the Connecticut line, turning south onto RI 94 across from Bowdish Reservoir. Follow RI 94 for 1.3 miles to a parking area beside a hunter checking station on the left. Signs indicate that this is the Durfee Hill Management Area.

Trail

Before walking, take a moment to look over the surrounding countryside. Below and to the right of the parking lot, as you face the checking station building, lies a shallow pond. It is picturesque in every season. In summer, it is decorated with water lilies and usually has swallows swooping above it. In spring and fall, the field in the foreground and the high, forested ridge on the far side of the pond add more color. In winter, the combination of snow and the deep green hemlocks produces an idyllic scene whether the pond is open, locked in ice, or covered with snow.

You will conclude your walk with a circuit of this pond, but begin by walking up the roadway, RI 94, to the left as you leave the parking lot. The part of the management area that includes the high ledges is on the opposite side of the road and will lead to the old gristmill and the second pond.

Stay on the paved road only 0.2 mile, until you reach a path on your right between utility poles 33 and 33½. As with other trails here, this is an unmarked path and is relatively narrow at its start.

Almost immediately, you can see the high rock wall looming through the pine trees on the right. This is the highest of several sheer cliffs in the area, and occasionally you will see climbers here practicing their techniques.

The path runs parallel to the wall for less than ¼ mile, until the wall dwindles and begins to flatten. Then the path curves to the left and joins a wider lane. Take this lane to the right. Now you are walking among taller pines, and the lane is often carpeted with pine needles.

The lane winds downhill, then runs along the edge of a brushy marsh. A couple of cutoffs go to the marsh, which often attracts swallows, kingbirds, warblers, and other songbirds. When you reach an open area, you can go a few steps to the right, onto an earthen dike that helped create the marsh, for an even better look at the marsh and its inhabitants, both birds and plants.

A trail runs across the dike and into the forest beyond, but for this walk, remain on the main lane as it curves left, away from the marsh. This is an easy, open, downhill segment. Again, ignore side trails; most were made by motorcyclists.

The shallow pond at Durfee is lovely in all seasons.

When the lane reaches a Y-junction, turn to the right for a detour to the gristmill and another lovely pond. Later, you will return and take the other fork.

By taking the right fork, you quickly pass a stone wall and an orange barway and emerge onto a dirt road. This road is virtually on the state line; if you went a few steps to your right, you would be in Connecticut. Instead, go to the left; the cottages at the waterway are in sight. There is only one cottage on each side of the road, the one on the left being on the shore of the pond and the one on the right, signed GRISTMILL COTTAGE, perched on the stream that tumbles out of the pond.

The dam and most of the stonework from what had been a mill are under the bridge. The views from the bridge are contrasting: a placid millpond on one side and a hurrying, splashing brook far below on the other. Both views are worth lingering a few moments.

When you are ready to resume your walk, go back up the road to the point where you came out of the woods and take the lane, now on your right, past the orange barway. Remain on the main lane; cycle paths to the right follow the pond but then run off state property. When you reach the Y trail junction you passed earlier, take the right fork.

This is a narrower trail than the lane but easy to follow. It curls to the left, mostly going uphill, and at one point passes a large rock outcropping on the right. This mass is not as high as the rock wall you passed earlier, but it's still worth a look. Shortly beyond the outcropping, the trail dips through a hemlock stand and reaches a wider lane. This is part of the lane you walked earlier. This time, turn to the right. In minutes, you will emerge (behind a guardrail) onto RI 94.

You could simply walk the highway to the left back to your car, but you have gone only 1½ miles. Instead, almost directly across the road you'll see another orange-barred lane, beside pole 35. Take this lane back into the forest. In moments you'll see a cemetery, just to the left of the trail, surrounded by a stone wall, an iron gate, and tall pines. Clean and clipped, this graveyard dates back to the 1820s.

Beyond the graveyard, the going gets a little tricky, with several side paths that can be confusing. It's best to stay on the main lane as it curves left just past the cemetery, running downhill, and then goes right to enter an open, sandy area. The lane ends in the open area, but if you walk the left edge of the clearing, you'll find a path leading downhill back into forest. This trail quickly reaches a T-junction; go left, and a brook will be on your right. In moments you'll reach an earthen dam and the pond you saw earlier from the parking lot. This spot provides great views of the water, the wood-duck houses to the right, the water lilies (in-season), and the fields across the way. Look also at the brook that runs out below the dam; chewed saplings and sticks show that beavers sometimes travel through here. In fact, beavers periodically dam up the culvert between the pond and the brook.

Again, you can shorten the outing by walking the left shore of the pond back to your car, but that area tends to be wet, and you would miss some of the finest sections of forest as well as close-up looks at the fields and old fruit trees that attract wildlide on the far side of the pond.

So cross the dam, to the right. Sighting down the right shore you may see a beaver lodge in the corner of the pond. The trail, however, goes uphill, away from the water. Soon you begin a long, sweeping curve to the left, and this is your longest climb of the day. When the path levels out, you are atop a ridge in a grove of hemlocks, some of which are of magnificent size and shape.

You are circling the pond but for most of this section you cannot see the water because of the dense foliage. The trail is easy to follow—it runs the crest of the ridge. Ignore all paths that run off to either side.

The descent is gradual, with some up-and-down going. Shortly after you begin seeing the pond again, the trail crosses a little brook and ends at an open field. Look over this field and those ahead carefully; I've seen deer here more than once. Sometimes these fields are planted in grain for the wildlife.

A tractor lane runs along the right edge of the fields. Take it. It will meander past the fields, small woodlots, old apple trees, and meadows all the way up to the parking lot at the hunter checking station. But don't be in a hurry to finish; this final segment is likely to be filled with wildflowers in spring and with birds at all times. And there's always the chance you'll see a fox or deer.

Walkabout Trail

Three choices of loops in one walk; pond views, hemlock groves, boulders, and a wildlife marsh

Hiking distance: 8 miles
Hiking time: 4 hours
Difficulty: Relatively easy, but with considerable
rocky footing

The Walkabout Trail is one of the old favorites of hikers in the northern part of Rhode Island, and it remains popular because it is still a delight. It offers not only a variety of features but also three loops that can make the walk as short as 2 miles or as long as 8 miles. The third loop is 6 miles.

All the loops begin and end together, near a beach on Bowdish Reservoir in the George Washington Management Area in Glocester. All offer good views of the reservoir and run along the edge of a campground. The longer trails ramble through dense woodlands and past another pond. The widest circuit, the 8-mile loop described here, also goes through a portion of adjacent Pulaski Park, running briefly on a cross-country ski trail, then circles through an impressive hemlock grove and visits a delightful wildlife marsh.

Most of the trail is relatively flat, but there are numerous areas of rocky footing that will require some care, and in a few places the path crosses low-lying areas that are likely to be muddy in wet periods. The trail is usually well maintained, and there are numerous wooden walkways over boggy spots and some trash barrels where the path crosses gravel roads. Early autumn, just after most of the campers have departed, is probably the best time to do this hike. From mid-October to the end of February, hunting season, hikers are required to wear orange hats or vests, as these loops are all in state management areas.

The Walkabout was cut and named by Australian sailors back in

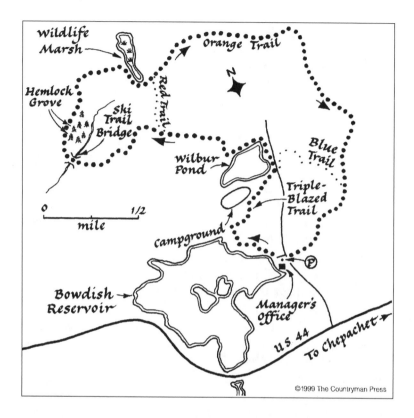

©1999 The Countryman Press

1965, while their ship, the *Perth,* was in dry dock in Newport. The name refers to the wanderings of the Australian Aborigines.

Access

To reach the trailhead, take US 44 to the George Washington Camping Area, about 4.5 miles west of Chepachet. Turn right onto the campground road and continue 0.3 mile until you reach a lane that runs to the left by the park office. Turn and park along this wide lane. Entry into the park requires a fee during the summer months.

Trail

All three loops of the Walkabout Trail begin behind a large sign and map outline just to the right of the reservoir beach. The 8-mile loop is blazed in orange, the 6-mile loop in red, and the 2-mile loop in blue. Through the early going and again at the end, trees will carry all three brightly painted blazes.

You begin by following the pond shoreline, walking through a dense but delightful forest of mountain laurel, pine, and hemlock. The path weaves among boulders, and there are several cutoffs to rocky points jutting out into the water. The footing is rocky, though, and exposed roots can trip you up, so pay some attention to what is at your feet.

In less than ½ mile, the trail swings to the right and runs along the edge of a camping area, several times skirting the rear of campsites. Soon you're walking on a woods lane, and where this lane joins a larger gravel road, the trail splits. The blue blazes go out onto the gravel road; the red and orange marks turn left back into forest, following the shoreline of a second pond. Unless you plan only a 2-mile walk, stay with the red and the orange blazes.

This pond is Wilbur Pond, a busy place in summer but tranquil and picturesque in other seasons. The trail, running through more hemlock groves, follows the shore for about ½ mile, going up and down several small hills and often running at the water's edge. Some camps can be seen across the pond, but your chances of finding ducks, geese, or other waterfowl here are excellent, especially in autumn.

At the end of a small cove, the trail breaks away from the pond and goes uphill, to the right, into an open, pleasant woodland with more undergrowth than is found in the hemlocks. In this section, the red trail breaks off to the right; take it if you're looking for a 6-mile walk. This connector segment will cross a gravel road and run past numerous stone walls and rock piles that show the area was once farmland. It then rejoins the orange trail, and the two run together again for the last 2-plus miles of the walk. However, the red trail misses the best hemlock groves, the ski trail, and the wildlife marsh.

Those continuing on the orange trail leave the rocky areas for a while, walking on an easy, flat path. You start crossing gravel roads (popular in winter as snowmobile trails) and enter an area where, as of this writing, a forest management study is being conducted. Many trees are marked with variously colored ribbons, and other trees have metal plates nailed to them. You'll also pass into Pulaski Park in this area, although no signs along the trail show the dividing line.

One of the open roads, about 3½ miles from your start, is marked with triangular red blazes, indicating that it is a ski trail originating at Peck Pond in Pulaski Park. For a short distance, you'll walk this road, going down a hill and then over a wide bridge. Just beyond the bridge, an orange arrow on a tree and a sign indicate that the Walkabout turns to the right while the ski trail goes ahead. The sign says the distance back to the GW (George Washington) Campground is 5 miles. Take heart; it's only about 4½.

Again walking on a path blazed only in orange, you are in an easy segment. The trail runs parallel to a gravel road for almost ½ mile before crossing the road (this lane is marked with yellow and blue-green ski blazes) and heading downhill into another grove of towering, impressive hemlocks. Soon the trail narrows considerably, and eventually you return to rocky and slightly hilly terrain. When you emerge from this section onto another gravel road, you're near one of the highlights of this walk.

As soon as you cross this road, you'll see the marsh off to your left. The trail runs along the shore for a short distance, then turns left at the open, grassy dike that created the marsh. You've now gone 5 miles, and this is a great place to take a rest break. The marsh attracts much wildlife, including swallows, kingfishers, wood ducks (which are lured by wooden nesting boxes installed on poles above the water), muskrats, and raccoons. Now beavers have joined the list. A lodge can be seen along the left shore, as you face the marsh from the dike, and other evidence of their presence can be found in cone-shaped stumps and chewed-off twigs.

When you are ready to resume the walk, cross the dike to the far end and return to the woods. Almost immediately, the trail splits. Stay left, with the orange blazes. In just over ½ mile, your path will be joined by the red trail coming in from the right. The walking is easy at first, then becomes more up-and-down and crosses several damp areas where you may have to pick your way, even in summer and fall, by stepping on rocks and exposed roots.

From the time the red trail rejoins your path, it is more than ½

The Walkabout Trail provides many good views of Bowdish Reservoir.

mile until you cross the next gravel road. Go straight across the road and you're entering the final segment. Here you'll see the largest boulders along the Walkabout, many of them covered with lichens or mosses. The trail gradually runs downhill into a lovely but damp area of big hemlock and laurel. One section of this wet area is equipped with hundreds of short logs lying crosswise, creating a miniature version of an old-fashioned corduroy road and serving as a walkway. When you reach the end of this walkway, you're at the foot of a rather steep hill.

Go up the hill and you'll see the blue trail coming in from the right. Now, once again following triple blazes, it's an easy ½-mile walk on a worn, mostly downhill path back to your car at the beach.

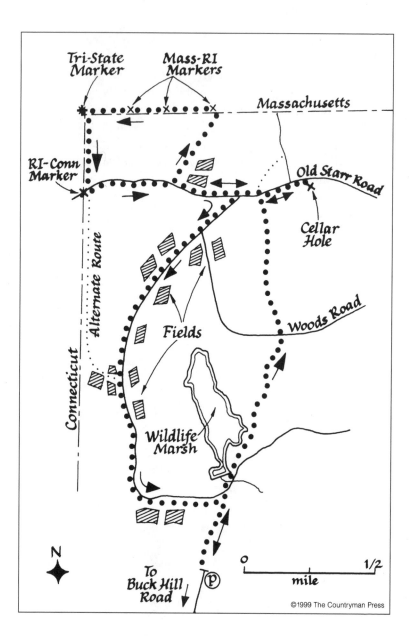

Tri-State Marker

Mass-RI Markers

Massachusetts

RI-Conn Marker

Old Starr Road

Cellar Hole

Connecticut

Alternate Route

Fields

Woods Road

Wildlife Marsh

N

To Buck Hill Road

P

0   1/2
            mile

©1999 The Countryman Press

Buck Hill

28

A search for a three-state marker in an area abounding in wildlife

Hiking distance: 5½ miles
Hiking time: 3–3½ hours
Difficulty: Moderately easy; mostly on open lanes, but some rocky footing on narrow paths

B uck Hill is a good place to visit if you want to combine walking with wildlife-watching, a bit of historical perspective, and a sense of accomplishment. After all, how often can you hike into three states in just a couple of hours? In fact, on this walk you'll find the granite post that marks the precise spot where Rhode Island, Connecticut, and Massachusetts meet.

The 2,000-acre Buck Hill State Management Area is in Burrillville, in the extreme northwestern corner of the state. And there has been plenty of "management" of this forest, including the construction of a large marsh and several tiny ponds and the cultivation of numerous small grain patches. The result has been an abundance of wildlife, including deer, foxes, raccoons, coyotes, rabbits, squirrels, ruffed grouse, wild turkeys, ducks, geese, owls, hawks, and dozens of species of songbirds. What you see may depend on when you go and how observant—and lucky—you are.

The 5½-mile route described here visits the marsh and some of the ponds and fields. It also cuts through a rocky forest, then follows ancient woods roads. You'll loop up to the Massachusetts state line, visit the tri-state boundary post, then follow the Connecticut line briefly before returning to Buck Hill's management roads. Shortcuts are possible, although they would eliminate the boundary post.

This loop is not to be confused with the northern terminus of the North South Trail (Walk 40), although NST walkers sometimes return along part of this route after reaching the Massachusetts line.

Buck Hill is probably most attractive in spring and fall, but remember that this area draws numerous hunters in October, November, and December.

Access

To reach the entrance road, take RI 100 north from Pascoag to Buck Hill Road and turn left. Watch your odometer; the entrance, beside a small sign, is 2.3 miles from the turnoff. You will pass a fire tower and a road to a Boy Scout camp on your left, then a rifle range on the right. The gravel access road is also on the right.

During most of the year you can drive only 0.3 mile from the paved road before being stopped at a barway. Once, you could drive directly to the marsh, but now the parking area has been moved. The management roads are open for driving during hunting season, but that is not a good time for hikers to be roaming the woods, so I suggest you wait until late winter or go in spring, summer, or early fall, even if you have to walk a little farther.

Trail

From the parking area, pass the gate and follow the entrance road straight ahead. One of the tiny ponds will be on your left, and the gravel road will be flanked with young pines. In about ⅓ mile you'll reach a lopsided crossroad; go straight ahead. (You'll be returning on the road at the left; the road going right eventually runs off state property.) Shortly after this crossroad, you'll see a small lane to the left going to an earthen dam and the marsh. Take a few minutes and look over this marsh, built to accommodate wildlife. Numerous wood-duck boxes have been erected over the water, and you'll likely see many birds here, ranging from swallows to ducks to herons. At times beavers have lived in the marsh, and other mammals visit it regularly. Hundreds of trees were drowned by the water, and their standing skeletons can give the place a slightly eerie appearance, particularly if you visit in twilight shadows, or at dawn, when mists rise around the old trees.

Continue following the lane around the right side of the marsh. After reaching another open spot that gives good views of the water, the lane dwindles to a narrow footpath blazed in yellow and enters a rocky forest. This path, strewn with rocks and slightly uphill, is one of the few segments of the hike not on open roads. It weaves for nearly ¾ mile before emerging onto a fire lane. You could turn left onto this lane for a shortcut (see map), but I recommend simply crossing the lane and staying on the narrow path. In this area you start seeing stone walls, reminders that this was once farmland, and in about ½ mile from the fire lane, you break out onto another road.

This is Old Starr Road, one of the earliest roadways in this area. Bounded on both sides by stone walls, it is worn deep into the forest floor. The yellow-marked footpath goes directly across this road and follows the state line to the northern terminus of the North South Trail. Unless that is your destination, I suggest turning right onto the road, going just 100 yards or so (passing another road on your left), and looking just off Old Starr Road on your right for a small cellar hole. This, legends say, was the home of the area's first white resident.

Now you're ready to search for the tri-state marker. Retrace your steps on Old Starr Road (heading west), past the spot where the yellow trail leaves the forest. The road dips through a low area, then reaches an intersection. A wide, grassy lane curves left, and just beyond, there is an opening on the right going into a field. Straight ahead is a narrow, overgrown path. Take it. In about 200 yards, the path opens considerably and you'll see a trail angling off to the right. Here you have a choice, because both the trail ahead and the path to the right can lead to the marker. For this walk, turn to the right; you'll return on the main trail.

This side trail angles back northeast for a short distance, going over a low ridge, then dropping slightly downhill. When you reach a side trail, on the left, look to the right for the first state marker, a stone post that says RI on one side and MASS on the other. Turn now and take this path to the left, and you'll soon pass two more, similar posts. Finally, this path climbs a small knoll where there is a small clearing. In the center is a 4-foot-high granite marker with names of all three states chiseled into its sides and the year 1883. This is a good place to rest; you've walked approximately 3½ miles.

Several trails run downhill from the marker; take the one that

One of the goals at Buck Hill is finding this tri-state boundary marker.

goes to the left of the path you were walking. It will drop through a low area and, in about ⅓ mile, reach another state boundary marker. This one is an upright fieldstone with RI on one side and C on the other, standing beside an old road. This road is the Old Starr Road you were walking earlier. Turn left from the marker and in about ⅓ mile you'll be back at the junction that took you to the Massachusetts line. Rewalk the narrow, overgrown path, then turn right onto the grassy lane that is Buck Hill's main access road.

(An alternative, if you prefer woods walking, is to go directly across Old Starr Road at the RI-C marker, following the state line. This is a straight but unblazed trail and a slightly shorter route back to the main management road. It is a pleasant enough walk but unremarkable. After ¾ mile, you reach a trail crossroad beside a yellow sign that says NO UNAUTHORIZED VEHICLES BEYOND THIS POINT, one of several such signs in the area. Turn left at the crossing and you'll soon reach a small grainfield, then another, and the road.)

If, like me, you'd rather have opportunities for seeing more wildlife, rewalk Old Starr Road back to the main access road and turn right. You'll pass small ponds with wood-duck houses, and numerous small clearings that are fields cut from the forest. Many are planted in grain for wildlife, and this area is your best chance for seeing deer, foxes, pheasants, turkeys, and other wild creatures. All fields are screened from the lane by trees, but each has an entrance lane that enables you to take a look. However, return to the main road each time to resume walking.

This long road eventually curves to the left, and the surface changes from grassy to sandy. The road takes you back to the gravel entrance road. Your car is to the right, but you might want to visit the marsh (now on your left) once more before leaving. It's a great place to rest and watch Buck Hill's wildlife.

Black Hut

A quiet forest walk with the birds and butterflies of northern Rhode Island

Hiking distance: 3 miles
Hiking time: 1½–2 hours
Difficulty: Easy; nearly all on flat and open lanes

I f you are looking for a quiet woods walk, with time and space to linger and look, give Black Hut a try. There you can roam for miles with little chance of running into other hikers, and maybe not any other people at all, unless it is hunting season.

The Black Hut Management Area in Burrillville is big, more than 1,500 acres, but has been overlooked by most Rhode Island outdoors enthusiasts. It does draw its share of hunters in late fall and early winter, and some trail bikers and horseback riders, but quite often hikers will have the huge forest all to themselves.

The only problem for hikers is that there are no marked trails at Black Hut, and while the old roads are easy and pleasant to walk, it's difficult to make a loop walk because most of the roads simply run off state property. Still, the 3-mile walk described here is terrific in that it visits a wildlife marsh, runs along small fields planted for the wild creatures, goes as far as a hurrying little stream, then circles through quiet forest. At all three turnaround points, the ambitious can explore farther if they wish, so the walk could be considerably longer than 3 miles or 2 hours.

In earlier editions of this book, I extended the Black Hut walk into other areas, but because those segments involved paved roads and extensive backtracking, I now recommend using this route.

Spring is probably the best season to visit Black Hut because of bird activity and wildflowers, and the chance of seeing other wild creatures.

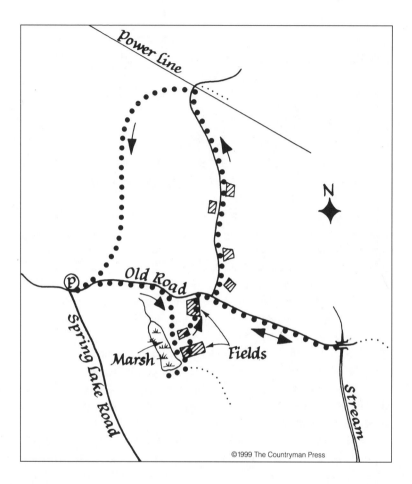

©1999 The Countryman Press

Access

Black Hut lies almost on the Massachusetts line in Burrillville. Take
RI 102 north from Chepachet or south from Slatersville, and take the
Glendale exit. In the tiny village of Glendale, look for Joslin Road,
which passes under RI 102, and take Joslin 0.1 mile north to the first
road on the left, Spring Lake Road. Follow Spring Lake 1.8 miles (it
eventually changes from pavement to dirt) to its end at a parking area
in the forest.

Trail

Barred lanes run both left and right from the parking area. The lane to the left once was a continuation of Spring Lake Road; now it is merely a narrow path. Take the wider lane running to the right.

Immediately beyond the barway, you'll see a path entering from the left; this will be your return route. For now, stay on the wide lane, which actually is an old roadway. This lane is somewhat curvy at its start and flanked by tall trees. There are many oaks and maples, with a healthy sprinkling of smaller trees such as sassafras, pine, and birch.

At ⅓ mile the road forks; go to the right. You soon are walking parallel to the wildlife marsh, on your right, but the views here are obscured by surging young pines. On the left you begin passing the first of the little grain plots planted for wildlife. Go slowly and quietly; deer, foxes, rabbits, birds, and butterflies use these fields. At ½ mile from your start, you reach the dike that helped create the marsh. Here, just to the right of the lane, are your best views of the marsh, which often attracts waterfowl and other birds as well as mammals, frogs, and other forms of wildlife.

It is tempting here to continue following the lane, which at the dike turns to the left, into the woods. You can follow it if you wish, but it eventually runs back out to Spring Lake Road, and you'd have to retrace your steps or follow the pavement back. Instead, go into the little field nearest the dike, look for an opening in the stone wall along the left side of the field, and follow the narrow path you find there. It quickly leads to a second, very small field. Go along the right edge of this field and you'll soon walk into a third field, which will lead you back to the entrance road. Or if finding your way through these little fields sounds too complicated, simply rewalk the lane beside the marsh to the junction you reached earlier.

The main roadway beyond the fields is perhaps the most pleasant part of Black Hut. This old road is lined with stone walls and shaded by tall, majestic trees. Walking this road also requires some backtracking, but here it is worth it. Shortly beyond the last field, you'll see another wide lane going off to the left; you'll walk it later. Stay on the main road for another ⅓ mile beyond the side lane and you'll reach the stream, crossed by a plank bridge. In spring, this

Shaded old lanes make walking Black Hut easy and pleasant.

stream usually runs high and fast and is extremely picturesque. The road continues beyond the bridge but soon runs off state property, so a turnaround here is recommended.

Return to the intersection with the other lane, now on your right. There are a couple of garden-size clearings along the first segment of this lane, and several more later. Like the main road, the lane is open and easy to walk, although there may be a few wet places. Just as you reach a power-line strip, you'll see a trail joining the lane from the left. This will be your return to the main road, but before turning, go a few steps farther and look over the clearing. Power-line strips are the closest thing to wild meadows in many areas now, and you may see bluebirds, hawks, and butterflies here as well as numerous species of wildflowers. Again, the ambitious can wander up and down the power line to their hearts' content before turning back.

When you are ready for the final leg, return to the trail junction just before the power line. This is more of a path than a lane but no less pleasant, unless it is a wet period; then you may be confronted with water pools. This path of just under 1 mile begins in pines and runs through varying stands of trees and bushes, including some mountain laurel. It has some minor ups and downs and you'll see several stone walls, some straight and solid, others erratic and tumbling. At one point the trail skirts the right end of a stone wall; when you pass this wall, you are nearing the main road. And when you reach this road, it's just a few steps to the right back to your car.

Fort Nature Refuge

A comfortable stroll with the wildlife in one of Rhode Island's newest public nature preserves

Hiking distance: 3¼ miles
Hiking time: 2 hours
Difficulty: Easy; nearly all on open, flat lanes

A quiet, beckoning oasis in North Smithfield awaits discovery by Rhode Island walkers. Officially the Florence Sutherland Fort & Richard Knight Fort Nature Refuge at Primrose Ledges, this onetime farm is now a surging forest turned over to wildlife.

Part of the refuge system of the Audubon Society of Rhode Island, the Fort Refuge consists of approximately 235 acres and includes three ponds, all made by the Fort family, who had created their own wildlife sanctuary before donating the property to Audubon in 1997. The 3¼-mile walk described here visits all three ponds, mostly on open, easy-to-walk lanes. The route includes two loops, blazed in blue, joined by a yellow-marked connector that crosses a power line. Shorter walks are available as well.

This is a nature preserve in the basic sense of the term, and the many facets of nature are the chief attractions. As you wander the lanes, you are likely to see many kinds of birds, possibly including wild turkeys and grouse, and you'll see tracks of deer if not the deer themselves. Coyotes and otters frequent the area as well, and depending on the season, you may find ducks and herons at the ponds, along with dragonflies, butterflies, frogs, turtles, and numerous wildflowers, including immense stands of water lilies.

Because it is an Audubon property, no hunting is allowed, so this is a good place to visit during autumn and winter for those who

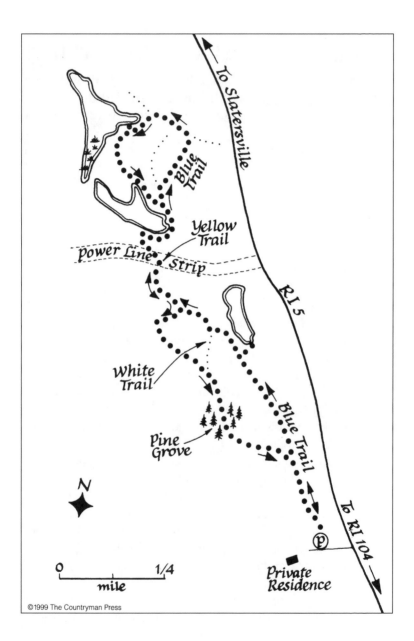

To Slatersville

Blue Trail

Yellow Trail

power Line strip

RI 5

White Trail

Blue Trail

Pine Grove

N

0   1/4
    mile

To RI 104

Ⓟ

Private Residence

©1999 The Countryman Press

are uncomfortable sharing state management areas with hunters. And because much of the forest at Fort is pine and hemlock, it is a particularly attractive place to walk in snow. The relatively flat lanes make it an excellent place for cross-country skiing as well as walking.

As with all Audubon Society refuges, visitors to Fort are asked to remain on the trails and to leave dogs at home.

Access

The Fort Nature Refuge is on RI 5 in North Smithfield. The entrance lane is 0.4 mile north of RI 5's intersection with RI 104, just beyond the Primrose fire station, or 3 miles south of the village of Slatersville. As you proceed up the lane, look for a grassy parking area and kiosk on the right. The entrance lane is gated beyond the parking lot because it leads to a private residence.

Trail

The trail begins just to the right of the kiosk among small pines. In moments you are on an old lane, one of the many tractor lanes used by the Fort family when they farmed the land and later made it into a wildlife sanctuary. As soon as you begin walking the lane, you'll see a blue-blazed path coming down a slope on the left; this will be your return route. For now, walk the flat, nearly straight lane that runs through dense forest. For much of this early part, the lane is flanked by tall trees. Where the trees are considerably smaller, you are passing former fields now returning to forest. Here, as throughout your walk, you are likely to see deer or coyote tracks on the path and perhaps flush a grouse or pheasant.

In just under ½ mile, you reach a cutoff path to the right. Take this for your first look at a pond. The short path ends at the shore. Approach quietly; this pond often harbors wood ducks and other waterbirds. In summer it is ringed with water lilies.

Back on the blue trail, you begin going slightly uphill as the trail curves left and then reaches a fork. A path blazed in white goes to the left; take it only if you want a very short walk. For this walk, remain on the blue trail. The lane is flanked in places by rocky ridges, and you'll cross a small brook on a low stone bridge. After passing a

Fort is a nature refuge in every sense of the term.

barred lane on the right, begin looking, also on the right, for the yellow-blazed connector path. Skipping the connector and the second blue loop will give you a walk of less than 2 miles, and you would miss two of the refuge's three ponds.

The yellow connector quickly takes you out of the forest into a strip cleared for a power line. Pause here and look around; these clearings often contain birds and wildflowers you cannot find in the forest. The trail crosses the strip and a motorcycle trail, then returns to forest on another old lane. Soon, though, it breaks off to the right into a dense hemlock thicket, then emerges in moments into a field returning to forest. This is a good opportunity to see what bushes and trees take over when a field is abandoned. At this writing, blueberries are among the old field's new inhabitants. There is a possibility that this field or one of the others may be cleared again in the future to add more habitat diversity for wildlife.

After running along the right edge of this old field briefly, the trail turns to the right and cuts through a second hemlock grove, angling downhill toward the second pond. After passing a group of glacial rocks called erratics, you drop down to the pond's shore. This pond has even more water lilies than the first, plus numerous frogs, turtles, and wood-duck nesting boxes.

Shortly beyond the shoreline opening, the yellow trail terminates at the beginning of the second blue loop. It's is a short loop, about ½ mile, and obviously you can go around either way. For this walk, go right. There are side trails and lanes here; ignore them and remain with the blue blazes. You'll soon reach a well-worn lane and curve to the left. Where the worn lane goes off to the right, through a barway, the blue blazes continue curving left. Now begin looking, on the right, for a cutoff to the third pond. This detour takes you to the pond's shallow end, a place decorated in spring and summer with blooming water plants and often sheltering herons and other birds.

From this pond, the trail curls through more fields-returning-to-forest, a great place for songbirds, and then skirts the edge of the second pond on its return toward the yellow connector trail. After backtracking on the yellow trail across the power line, you return to the first blue loop. Now turn right.

This is an easy, pleasant section with surging ferns on the ground beneath tall pines. The trail swings left and gradually climbs a low ridge. Here, on the left, you see the largest boulders of this walk. The lane continues running through the pine grove until it reaches the junction with the white trail, coming in from the left. For the next ¼ mile or so, you are walking with a grove of pines on your left and mixed woods on the right. When the trail turns left and angles over a ridge, you are nearing the end of your walk. This path emerges onto the grassy lane you walked earlier. The parking lot and your car are just to the right.

Diamond Hill

A short trip to the top of a cliff and back down through a lovely park

Hiking distance: 2 miles
Hiking time: 1½ hours
Difficulty: Strenuous in places, fairly easy in others

Walking the Diamond Hill Trail continues to change, but a visit to this state park in Rhode Island's northeastern corner remains worth the effort. It's still a delightful place.

Several years ago, both sides of steep, rocky Diamond Hill sported skiing operations, and a hiking trail crossed the hill's summit, curled around a reservoir, and wandered into Massachusetts. When the ski business fell apart, the state-owned side of the hill was developed into a popular, family-oriented park. The opposite side, the one near the reservoir, was developed in another way; it sprouted numerous condominiums.

So the walking has changed, too. Now this walk is barely 2 miles long, but it still loops through the park. It begins with a brief walk up one of the old ski slopes, then goes through a section of forest, climbs to the top of a high cliff, runs along the cliff's rim, which provides panoramic views of the area, and finally descends along other old ski slopes.

Bring along a lunch, but there is no need to lug it all the way to the cliff. The walk will probably take less than 2 hours, and a pavilion, a pond, and picnic tables in the park make it an inviting place for a leisurely lunch after your hike.

The route described here scrambles up the cliff, but there is an alternate path to the top for those who prefer not to tackle an exposed area where stone can be loose or, in wet weather, a bit slippery. The only blazes of any kind in the park are small metal disks that mark a route up the cliff and along the top of the hill.

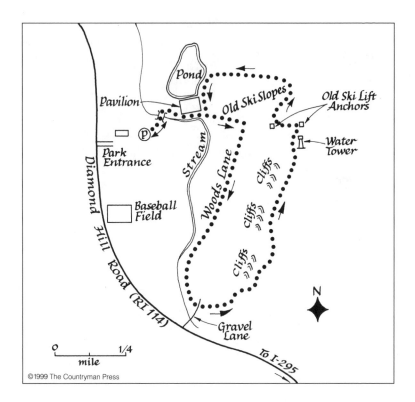

©1999 The Countryman Press

Access

Take I-295 into Cumberland, exit on RI 114 (Diamond Hill Road), and follow the signs 4 miles to Diamond Hill State Park, which is on your right. The parking lot is very large.

Trail

Look for the pavilion and the old ski slopes beyond, then begin walking by following a path along the right edge of the ski slope at the right. Higher, you'll see the open strip being claimed by young pine trees. The slope is not particularly steep or difficult to walk. When you are a little more than halfway to the top, where the grassy terrain gives way to stones, look for a path going off into the woods at the right. Take it.

(This path will run to the cliff trail. If you are not interested in making that climb, remain on the ski slope path. It will take you to the rim in an easier manner, and you can then visit the overlooks, most of which will be to your right.)

The woods path is open and pleasant, passing beside large trees and virtually all downhill for several hundred yards. When it flattens out, you'll find yourself walking at the base of the hill, on your left, and parallel to an old railroad bed, on your right. Continue until the path emerges into an open area where several trails turn left, up the 150-foot cliff. There will be a gravel lane on your right, running in from RI 114.

Look over the paths carefully; you want a trail blazed with small metal disks nailed to trees. The disks mark this route as the Appalachian Mountain Club's long Warner Trail, which runs all the way from Canton, Massachusetts. The trail ends at RI 114.

The disk trail curls to the right at the foot of the graffiti-marred cliff, appearing to go off into the woods, but quickly veers back and continues to the top. It is relatively steep and mildly strenuous but not very dangerous, if care is taken, and you'll reach the top in minutes.

Take some time to enjoy the views. Spread out below is a residential area, Diamond Hill Village, and beyond are hills and forests. The foliage is often spectacular in autumn.

When you are ready to resume walking, stay with the disk trail. Numerous other paths run all across the summit, but the disk trail is best. It follows the rim, for the most part, and allows detours to the rocky overlooks. The disks aren't always easy to see, however, so go slowly.

The trail will curve away from the rim and take you to a water tower, installed for the condominium project below you on the right. Go around the left side of the fenced-in tower, and almost immediately you'll see large concrete blocks that once anchored the ski lifts. From these blocks, go left (again, the disks are hard to see) several yards to another concrete platform. This is the spot where skiers dismounted for their runs down the hill. Now saplings and young trees are thriving here; they nearly obscure the view.

From the platform, the disk trail goes to the right a short distance,

The trail on the cliff overlooks Diamond Hill Village.

then turns left down a gravel lane. (Going to the right on this lane will allow a look at the condos and the reservoir beyond.) When the gravel lane to the left forks, you have a choice. You can stay with the left fork, go over a ridge, and descend on a ski slope. Or you can follow the disks around on the right fork and then down another former ski run. It doesn't matter very much: Both slopes lead down to the center of the attractive park, the pond, the pavilion, and all those places to enjoy your picnic.

Lincoln Woods

A leisurely stroll around an idyllic pond

Hiking distance: 2¾ miles
Hiking time: 1–1½ hours
Difficulty: Easy; mostly on paved road

Lincoln Woods is a large old park close to Rhode Island's population centers, and perhaps because of that it is often overlooked by "serious" walkers, particularly those who prefer the solitude of so-called wilderness. To my mind, such people are missing a good thing.

It's true that there is no wilderness here, but on this easy loop around the park's focal point, picturesque Olney Pond, you'll stroll 2¾ miles and see lovely sights. You can walk a road all the way if wish, or you can, as I suggest here, cut through forest on several occasions. Depending on the season, you may also want to try your hand at fishing, take time for a picnic, or even end your walk with a refreshing swim. There are a great many other paths and trails through the woods, but none is blazed, and sorting them out can be confusing, so walking around the pond is the recommended route.

The park is a busy place in summer, but in other seasons there is plenty of room for walking. Autumn is probably the ideal time to visit, when the foliage around the pond is at its finest. You are not likely to see unusual wildlife in the park, but ducks, herons, kingfishers, and other waterbirds are common, as are songbirds. And you'll probably see squirrels and chipmunks, particularly in fall. Also, there is the sport of people-watching. Along your route you will meet other walkers, joggers, picnickers, bicyclists, and families strolling with young children. In some areas there may be anglers, horseback riders, orienteering athletes, and sunbathers.

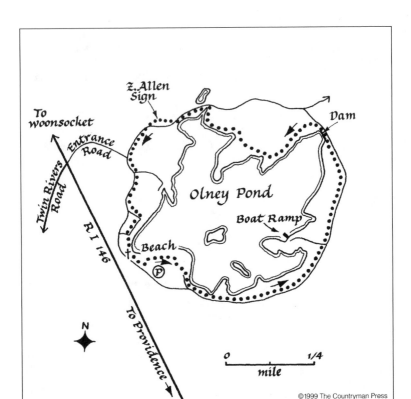

Access

The park is in Lincoln, almost within sight of Providence, Pawtucket, North Providence, and Central Falls. Access from both the north and south is provided by RI 146 via Twin Rivers Road. In summer a fee is charged for entering, but there is no charge from Labor Day to Memorial Day.

From the entrance, drive to the right past the beach area and park in the lot near the complex of modern buildings. The beach, food concession, and rest rooms (open only in summer) make this a good place to end a walk.

Trail

From the parking lot, cross a wooden bridge to the buildings, then begin the hike by following a walkway of fine gravel to the right. It initially leads away from the water but quickly returns to the shore and joins a paved road. When this road is open to auto traffic, it is one-way and you're walking with the flow.

The road alternately goes down to the very edge of the pond, then climbs many feet above it. You are never far from the water, and the views of the pond, with its rocky shoreline, wooded islands, and numerous coves, are delightful. Most of the trees above you are oaks, making this an especially attractive area in late October and early November, but the understory includes such plants as sassafras and dogwood, which color somewhat earlier.

At a gravel road to the left, you have gone about ¾ mile. Just beyond, the road climbs again and leaves the pond briefly. Off the road, to the right, is a string of houses, a reminder of just how close this park lies to residential areas.

When the road drops downhill again, you will reach a concrete wall and a small dam, often crowded with people fishing. You are now a little less than halfway around the pond. Just beyond the dam you can leave the pavement, swinging left into the woods. Numerous paths run through here but there is little chance of getting lost. The pond is on one side and the road on the other. The best rule is to follow the shore.

You will reach a spot where it seems that there are two ponds separated by a narrow strip of land, and a trail runs onto the strip. That path, however, is a dead end, so go on by, walking what is here a wide and worn path at the water's edge. The trail splits often; keep taking the left fork, following the shore. There are huge boulders and ledges here, features that might make you forget you're in a "city park"—unless you can smell hot dogs being grilled at the picnic tables along the road.

The path snakes between the boulders and emerges onto the road almost directly across from a very small pond. Turn left and follow the road a short distance as it curves right. Just around the bend is a sign honoring Zachariah Allen, who, back in 1820, began the first silviculture experiment near here, planting trees to bring worn-out land back to life.

Most of the woods on the pond side of the road in this area are boggy, so continue following the pavement. You'll soon pass the entrance road you drove earlier, then a fishing access road on your left. Stay on the main park road until you reach a parking lot in a grove of pine trees on the left. Walk along the rear of the parking lot, then cut across a narrow strip of woods to a grassy slope where there are many picnic tables and toilet facilities. To the right is an ancient cemetery surrounded by a thick stone wall. Take a moment to look it over; this is the resting place of the Olney family, for whom the pond was named. Some of the tombstones date to the 1700s.

When you are ready to continue walking, go down the slope to the water's edge, then follow a path to the right. It will take you around the final corner of the pond to the beach. Your walk will be finished, and it will be time for a plunge or a picnic.

Ruecker Wildlife Refuge

A short walk along the Sakonnet River to see birds and fiddler crabs

Hiking distance: 1½ miles
Hiking time: 1–1½ hours
Difficulty: Easy; almost the entire loop is on flat, easy paths,
and wooden walkways take you over wet areas

This walk is a little jewel. Looping through the Emilie Ruecker Wildlife Refuge, it is only 1½ miles long on an easy-to-walk path. If you like birds and fiddler crabs, you are likely to be fascinated nearly every step of the way.

The refuge, located on the salty shores of the Sakonnet River in Tiverton, was a 30-acre farm before the owner, Emilie Ruecker, donated it to the Audubon Society of Rhode Island in 1965. Now, thanks to its natural attributes—shallow marshes, small fields, and upland woodlots—and Audubon management, the refuge attracts a wide variety of bird life, particularly during the spring and fall migrations. The fiddler crabs and some unusual rock formations add to the attraction, but for most walkers it is the birds that make the trails of Ruecker so inviting.

Access

Follow RI 77 south from the village of Tiverton about 3 miles to Sapowet Road. Turn right and drive less than 0.5 mile to the refuge, which is on the right. The sign and small parking lot are rather inconspicuous, so look carefully.

Trail

As soon as you arrive, you will start hearing birds. In spring and early summer, you may hear quail whistle from the surrounding farms, and

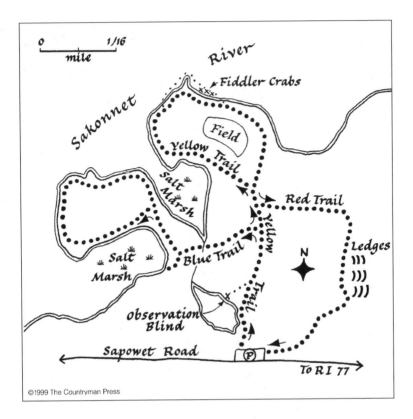

warblers and catbirds call from within the sanctuary's dense growth of bushes and small trees. In fall, migrating swallows—sometimes in the thousands—gather in this area before heading south. In winter, a feeding station near the entrance, operated by the Audubon staff, draws chickadees, nuthatches, and nearly every other bird that usually winters in the state. Over the course of a year, about 150 species of birds frequent this little refuge.

The main trails are called the Yellow, Blue, and Red Trails, but they are not blazed in the conventional way with paint spots on trees. Instead, signs and arrows point the way. One short side trail still has the old blazes painted in white. Even with frequent stops to observe the birds, you can easily walk all these trails in 1 to 1½ hours.

From the parking lot, take the Yellow Trail. It starts beside a wooden kiosk, where trail maps are usually available. The trail runs through a small grove of cedars and hemlocks then quickly comes to a path, with faded white blazes, going left, just before a stone wall. This path leads to an observation blind at a shallow pond. In most seasons, you can find herons, egrets, ducks, and perhaps bitterns, sandpipers, and other birds here.

Beyond the hemlock grove, you enter the old farm fields, now overgrown with bushes, many of which produce berries that attract numerous birds. Several benches along the trails invite you to slow down and enjoy the bird activity. Catbirds are abundant here, along with mockingbirds, thrashers, orioles, thrushes, and goldfinches. In early spring, you may be able to see and hear the mating dance of woodcocks in the small fields kept open.

When you reach a sign for the Blue Trail loop, go left for a look at the salt marshes. The first segment takes you over a narrow brook, then onto a small peninsula. Short side trails lead to the shore for good views of the shallow water, which often draws herons, egrets, and swans. Tiny flowers called trailing arbutus can be found along the path in spring, and dense shadbush and bayberry add color when in flower. Later they supply berries for birds such as cedar waxwings, cardinals, and titmice.

When you complete the loop, return to the main trail, and you soon reach a major trail junction. Pass the Red Trail on your right (you'll take it later), and at a Y-intersection, take the left fork. This path, still part of the Yellow Trail, circles a larger peninsula, going all the way around an open field where birdhouses have been installed for bluebirds. This field is also where woodcocks put on their show on April evenings. The Yellow Trail runs a few yards back from the shore for the most part, but several side paths enable you to go down to the sand, where you are likely to find fiddler crabs in summer. Hundreds of tiny holes in the sand betray their presence, and on warm, sunny days you may see hundreds of them scurrying across the beach or hiding just inside their burrows. For many walkers, especially those with small children, the fiddlers may be the highlight of a visit to Ruecker.

After you finish the Yellow Trail loop, take the Red Trail, now

The salt marsh at Ruecker is a haven for wading birds.

going off to your left. Here you enter the deepest woods in the refuge, although stone walls show that this area, too, once was farmland. Taller hardwoods are mixed with pines and cedars, and you will notice unusual boulders scattered about. These rocks appear to consist of small pebbles cemented together; local residents call the boulders puddingstone. This sedimentary bedrock, estimated to be 250 million years old, is found in few places other than the Narragansett Bay basin. A similar, though larger, mass formed Hanging Rock in the Norman Bird Sanctuary (Walk 35).

The trail winds along a low ridge of the puddingstone before curving right, back toward the refuge interior. It then runs through a dense, damp section equipped with wooden walkways, and too soon emerges at the parking lot. But don't hurry off; sometimes the trees around the parking area offer another excellent variety of birds.

Simmons Mill Pond

A leisurely walk through a forest crafted for birds and other wildlife

Hiking distance: 3½ miles
Hiking time: 2½–3 hours
Difficulty: Easy; entire route is on open, flat lanes

Not many walkers know the Simmons Mill Pond Management Area yet, and those who have never been on its lanes are missing a delightful experience. Among the newer state properties, it offers miles of lanes and old roads, extensive woodlands, numerous ponds, and some open fields. Most of the lanes are flanked by stone walls and towering trees. Add it all up, and Simmons is an ideal place to walk in spring, when bird activity is highest, or in fall, when the foliage show is at its best.

The 400-acre property in Little Compton has been catering to wildlife for many years. Back when it was private property, its owners, particularly Bill Chace, created a wildlife sanctuary by building a network of ponds in the forest. Now the ponds, connected by open lanes, attract ducks, geese, ospreys, herons, swallows, and numerous other birds, as well as such mammals as deer, minks, foxes, muskrats, and raccoons. The largest pond, the 18-acre millpond for which this area is named, is well known to local anglers, but walkers often have most of the property to themselves.

My wife and I have had some great wildlife experiences here, including observing a curious baby fox that kept popping out of its den to watch us, and an attack by an irate mother grouse that came at us when we apparently walked too near her nest or brood of chicks.

There are no blazed trails at Simmons, and many of the lanes run at confusing angles (some simply run off the property, so care must be taken when visiting for the first time). The route described here, which hits the best features and represents the easiest loop, is about 3½ miles long. For those who want a longer walk, there are several other lanes

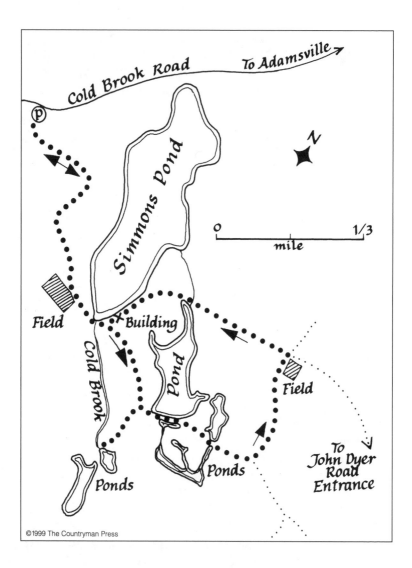

that can be explored, although in most cases you'll have to turn back when you reach the boundaries of the state property.

As a state management area, Simmons is subject to hunting season regulations, including the wearing of orange from October to the end of February. Spring, however, is probably the best time to visit.

Access

Simmons has two entrances. For this walk, use the main parking lot on Cold Brook Road. Take RI 179 or RI 81 into Adamsville, then take Cold Brook Road about 1.5 miles southwest to the entrance, on the left. A smaller parking lot is on John Dyer Road south of Adamsville.

Trail

For the first ½ mile, the trail is a gravel lane that runs through a mixed forest of midsize trees and dense underbrush. If you visit in spring, you are likely to find numerous birds as soon as you begin walking, most likely thrushes, towhees, warblers, catbirds, and ovenbirds. While the lane is barred to vehicle travel, it is easily wide enough for a car and walking is easy.

You'll pass a lane angling back to the right (one of the dead-end roads) and then see an open field on the right. This is one of the fields planted in grain each year for wildlife. You may see or hear pheasants or quail here, and probably will find orioles or thrashers in the trees surrounding the field.

Just beyond the field, the lane runs across a dike that helped create the largest pond. To your left is the 18-acre pond, and chances are you can see geese and ducks on the water, and perhaps an osprey or two hovering above or perched in trees along the shore. This is also where you are likely to see fishermen. On the right side of the dike bridge, Cold Brook spills down through the woods.

Beyond the bridge, an inviting lane breaks off to the left, following the shore, and you can see a building at the water's edge. You could follow that lane now, but for this walk, go straight; you'll return on the lane by the building. It's a great place to rest after your walk.

The main entrance road, after leaving the large pond, is more grass than gravel. It curves to the right, passing beneath tall trees that provide shade in summer and colorful foliage in autumn. In ¼ mile you reach another fork. If you wish, take the lane going to the right for a look at some of the smaller ponds, but then *return to the intersection and resume walking the main road.* Shortly beyond the intersection, you reach a small bridge with a high dike on the left and several small

The deck of this abandoned building is a great place to linger.

ponds on the right. Go up on the dike for a good view of the second largest pond on the property. Again, you are likely to see waterbirds of several varieties here. Paths to the right beside the bridge enable you to look over the smaller ponds.

Once past the pond area, the road makes a long, sweeping curve to the left. Throughout this area, you'll find an interesting mixture of trees, including the relatively rare holly. Stone walls meander through the forest in some areas, and in some sections they flank the road. You'll soon see another road breaking off to the right, through an opening in a stone wall. That route is good for exploring—it leads to a brook, some wetland areas, and more wild forest—but it can be confusing with several more branchings, and it eventually runs off state land, so you'll have to return. For this walk, stay on the main road, turning left at the junction with the side road.

This next section is perhaps the most idyllic part of Simmons. Stone walls line the road, and tall trees meet overhead. It was here that the female grouse rushed out and pecked at our boots. Most of the time, the birds are in the trees and bushes. When you reach a small open field on your right, look to the left side of the road. You'll find a stone-lined well, capped with a large round stone, and a series of small, stone-walled enclosures in the woods, possibly holding pens for livestock in another era.

Just beyond the field is still another crossroad. The main road runs straight ahead and beckons with its tall trees and stone walls, but it quickly reaches the property boundary. The lane to the right, the least worn of the four, goes to the John Dyer Road parking lot, a distance of about ⅓ mile. To continue this loop back to the millpond, turn to the left.

There are more side lanes leading off from this road; ignore them. In minutes, you reach a point where water crosses the road, sometimes in a trickle, sometimes in a cascade. Large stones on the left side are usually enough for you to cross without getting your feet wet. The pond on the left is the same one you saw earlier when you climbed the high dike at the series of ponds.

From this point, it is only a matter of minutes until you reach the building on the shore of Simmons Mill Pond. Once a retreat for the property owners, it was later used briefly as an education center. More recently, it has been boarded up. However, a deck at the rear of the building remains a great place to linger awhile and look over the pond. When you are ready to leave—and if you can tear yourself away—simply walk around the end of the pond to the bridge and retrace the ½ mile to your car.

Norman Bird Sanctuary

The famed Hanging Rock, other stone ridges, and an abundance of birds

Hiking distance: 3½ miles
Hiking time: 2–2½ hours
Difficulty: Easy on the flat trails, fairly strenuous on the ridge climbs

The Norman Bird Sanctuary, along the coast in Middletown, just east of Newport, stands out among Rhode Island walking places. It is one of the few places that charge a fee for entering, but some of its other qualities can make you feel the place is well worth the cost.

Norman, a privately owned property, has a natural history museum, there are usually live hawks or owls or other birds on the premises, recovering from injuries, and it is truly a sanctuary for birds of all kinds. You may see as many species on these trails as on any in this book. Also, rock hounds will love the place for its outstanding examples of conglomerate called puddingstone.

The trails wander back and forth over the refuge's 450-plus acres, and on the 3½-mile walk described here, you will travel three parallel yet distinct ridges. One leads to the famed Hanging Rock, from which you can see over Gardiner Pond and the ocean beach. Another offers views of Nelson Pond, its waterfowl, and a mansion beyond. Other trails pass through forests and around swamps, and one runs through an area managed for woodcocks. The ambitious can explore more of the sanctuary's trails, including one that climbs a fourth ridge. In all, Norman offers 8 miles of trails, many of which connect and reconnect several times.

© 1999 The Countryman Press

Access

To reach the sanctuary from the west side of Narragansett Bay, cross the Newport Bridge, take RI 138, and continue straight east, via Miantonomi Avenue and Green End Avenue, until you reach Third Beach Road. Go right (south) onto Third Beach Road less than 1 mile. The refuge is on the right.

From the east side of the bay, take RI 138 south to Mitchells Lane, turn left, and drive 2 miles to an intersection, then bear right onto Third Beach Road. Norman is 1 mile farther on the right.

The sanctuary is closed on Mondays except holidays. The admission fee covers use of the trails as well as access to the exhibits.

Pick up a trail map, which provides information on side trails not included here.

Trail

The walk starts behind the refuge buildings. Few trails here are blazed in the usual manner—paint splotches on trees—but there are numerous signs to keep you from getting lost. Follow the main entrance path downhill, past the first signs for side trails (the Woodland Trail and the Woodcock Trail), and take the Quarry Trail going to the left. You'll end this walk on the Woodland and Woodcock paths.

The Quarry Trail runs first along an open field, then turns right to the site of the old slate quarry, now often resembling a narrow pond on the left side of the path. Along the way you pass a side path, going right, named the Indian Rock Trail because it visits a quartz outcropping where Native Americans were said to make arrowheads. Just beyond the quarry pond, turn left onto the Blue Dot Trail, one of the paths blazed with paint. This open, grassy path runs through woods to a T-intersection. Turn left, and in moments you are crossing low ridges with stone walls, and then you will be walking parallel to the high stone ridge that leads to Hanging Rock.

There are several side paths that you could take to the top of the ridge, but they involve steep climbs. It is easier to remain on the Blue Dot Trail until its end, which is a more gradual ascent to the ridge. This ridge appears to be made up almost entirely of puddingstone. This fascinating rock mass, formed aeons ago, is composed of countless granite pebbles seemingly cemented together. Puddingstone, while relatively rare elsewhere, is common throughout the Narragansett Bay basin, but there may be no other place where it is as prominent as at Norman.

Once you climb the ridge, turn left, toward Hanging Rock. You are walking above the surrounding trees. The walking is relatively easy, but care must be taken because the rocks are not smooth, and the footing can be slippery when wet. The path ends abruptly at Hanging Rock, which seems to hang over the surrounding countryside. Pause awhile and take in the views. Below, to the left, is Gardiner Pond, where geese and ducks often congregate in fall. Beyond the pond is the Sachuest Point National Wildlife Refuge (see Walk 14, *More Walks and Rambles in Rhode Island,* Backcountry Publications), as well as the Atlantic Ocean and a public beach. Ahead is Newport and its shoreline, plus the stone tower of St. George's School. Below, to the right, is a marshy area, and beyond, another rocky ridge.

When you are ready to resume walking, retrace your steps along the ridge, past the point where you climbed up. The trail follows the crest, then descends to a trail intersection. Turn left. In a few yards you reach another junction with signs indicating the Valley Trail (which dead-ends at the marsh you saw from Hanging Rock), the Red Fox Trail, and the Grey Craig Trail. Take the Red Fox, which quickly splits. Now go on the left fork, which climbs the second ridge. It is about as high as Hanging Rock ridge but not quite as exposed. Cedars and other small trees grow through the cracks, although most of the plant life is twisted from constant buffeting by the wind. I remember walking this trail in November one year, and it seemed that every robin in Rhode Island had gathered here, feeding on cedar berries, before heading south. Often cedar waxwings, catbirds, kingbirds, and various sparrows and warblers dally in this area, too.

You'll also see a low stone wall wandering along the ridge, sometimes on one side, sometimes on the other. The top of a narrow rock ridge seems a strange place for such a wall.

When you reach the end of the ridge, the path curls down to the right. It then narrows considerably as it enters a tiny valley. Again, the trail splits. Turn left at the fork, taking a wooden walkway over a damp area, and climb the third ridge. This path is called the Nelson Pond Trail for the pond that lies at its base. The climb is short but steep. Now you are heading back toward the interior of the refuge. Below is Nelson Pond, and there are some good overlooks. The best viewing spots, however, are farther along the trail, after it runs through woods briefly and then returns to a rocky summit above the shallower backwaters of the pond. At migration time, you are likely to see geese, ducks, and perhaps loons and other waterfowl here. Some ducks remain throughout the summer, when you also should see swans and shorebirds of several kinds. Across the water stands

Hanging Rock is the most famous feature of the Norman Bird Sanctuary.

Grey Craig, an impressive mansion built in the 1920s. The outcroppings are good places to linger.

When the trail descends, it curls into the woods around a tiny pond—no more than a water hole—and returns to the Red Fox Trail junction you passed earlier. You have now walked about 2¾ miles, and could return to your car by continuing straight ahead. Or you can turn left onto the Grey Craig Trail. It would take you over a brook and up to a fourth ridge before bringing you back, and would extend the hike to about 4½ miles instead of 3½. For this walk, go straight ahead at the intersection, taking the wooden walkways. Follow the main path to a bridge and grassy dike at a shallow, rocky pond called Red Maple Swamp. This is a good spot from which to see swallows, dragonflies, and other creatures of the wetlands. Benches here may entice you into lingering before finishing the walk.

After crossing the dike, you could simply go back uphill to the buildings and your car, but I recommend turning left onto a path called the Woodland Trail. It runs through open, pleasant woods with numerous stone walls and boulders. Pass up the first major trail to the right but take the second, the Woodcock Trail, for the walk through woods and an overgrown field. The first time I walked here, I nearly stepped on a woodcock that had been probing for worms on the path. I haven't seen one here since, but I keep looking.

The trail ends at a small family graveyard. Turn right, following a lane along an open field, and in minutes you are back at the refuge headquarters.

Cliff Walk

Following Newport's shoreline bluff for ocean views and marvelous mansions

Hiking distance: 6¼ miles
Hiking time: 3 hours
Difficulty: Easy much of the way; considerable rocky
footing in the last mile before the turnaround

Sooner or later, every Rhode Island walker, and many a visitor to the state, has to try Cliff Walk. It is the state's most famous trail, a 3¼-mile walkway that follows part of the Newport shoreline, beginning at Easton Beach. For the entire distance, you have the sea on one side and the magnificent mansions of another era on the other.

In summer, this is a crowded walk, with numerous tourists using it not only for the ocean scenes but also to get a free look at the mansions, among the most lavish homes ever built in America. The trail runs behind dozens of these 60- and 70-room "cottages" built in the late 1800s, when Newport was the playground of the Vanderbilts and Astors, the Whartons and Belmonts, and other leaders of industry and finance. Many of these mansions, which face Bellevue Avenue, are now open in warm-weather months as museum-like relics of a gilded age.

A sparkling spring or crisp autumn day might be best for this walk, not only because the trail is crowded in summer but also because heat tends to smudge the sea views. There is virtually no shade for the entire 3¼ miles, and most of the walkway is concrete or stone, so a beating sun can make the hiking too hot.

If you walk the entire distance, you have to return, of course. You could simply retrace your steps, but there are other alternatives. A one-way walk is possible by leaving a vehicle on Ledge Road, just before the trail's end. Parking is banned at the end of Ledge Road, but there are a few spaces farther up. Another solution, for those who

don't want to do Cliff Walk in both directions, is just to walk back to Easton Beach on the city streets. This way you can see the front of some of the mansions you passed behind as well as those on the opposite side of Bellevue Avenue. Returning to your start in this way makes a walk of about 6¼ miles and provides different perspectives, many shady trees, and several shops as well as the famed Tennis Casino and International Tennis Hall of Fame.

Be aware that if you are committed to walking the entire shoreline, the final segment along the cliff is over large and potentially difficult rocks. The trail also takes a pounding from the elements, including the crashing surf, and therefore suffers frequent damage.

Access

To reach the start of Cliff Walk, take RI 138 into Newport, turn south onto RI 138A or RI 214, and continue to Memorial Boulevard. Turn right and you will quickly reach the state-owned Easton Beach, where you can park. Or you can take Memorial Boulevard east from the wharf area of downtown Newport. There is room for several cars on the street along the beach. Parking is free in the off-season; meters are in operation in summer. The beach parking lot also carries a fee in summer, but is free the rest of the year.

If you are leaving a car at Ledge Road, follow Memorial Boulevard uphill past the start of Cliff Walk, turn left onto Bellevue Avenue, and drive past the mansions. Just after the road makes a sharp turn right, look for Ledge Road on your left.

Many walkers also begin Cliff Walk by parking at the end of Narragansett Avenue, which runs off Bellevue. Beginning here means skipping the first segment of the trail, but parking sometimes is easier, and you would still include most of the route's highlights.

Trail

The trail begins, uphill from Easton Beach, behind a restaurant called Cliff Walk Manor. You quickly rise high above the sea. The path here is a sidewalk that twists and turns as it follows the shore. For the most part, fences or hedges, or both, line the right side. On the left is the ocean. To the far left, across a cove, you can see Middletown, Easton Point, and Sachuest Point.

When you reach the first street (Narragansett Avenue) coming in from the right, you are at Forty Steps. Originally a natural rock formation that provided access to the water, it was a gathering place in Newport's Gilded Age for the servants who worked in the mansions. The steps have been replaced many times, and now there is a concrete stairway with steps bearing the names of benefactors. Above the stairway is an observation deck that also serves as a memorial, with several names inscribed in the stones. This is where many walkers begin and end their visit to Cliff Walk.

Beyond Forty Steps you can see many large buildings on the right; most of them are now part of Salve Regina University. Here

Cliff Walk has the ocean on one side and mansions on the other.

you also encounter the first of many short stairways built into the trail. When you reach a permanently open iron gate, you are behind The Breakers, the Italian-style palace Cornelius Vanderbilt commissioned in 1895. A rose hedge, a wrought-iron fence, and a vast lawn separate the trail from the mansion, but several breaks in the hedge enable you to marvel at the awesome size of the 70-room "cottage."

After passing a second iron gate and several more immense homes, the trail turns and climbs a few steps between cement and brick walls. Through this section, the trail surface is sometimes asphalt, sometimes stone, sometimes dirt. Behind a high white wall on the right is Rosecliff, the famed mansion used in filming the movie *The Great Gatsby*. Unfortunately, not much of Rosecliff can be seen from the trail.

Perhaps the most photographed feature on Cliff Walk looms a few hundred yards ahead. This is a Chinese-style teahouse, standing almost directly above the trail, that was used by Mrs. Otto Belmont for entertaining when she resided at Marble House. You pass almost under the pagoda through a curving tunnel. The trail then swings left and passes through another short tunnel in a rocky ridge called Sheep Point.

After the tunnels, you leave sidewalks behind for good. The path is gravel and dirt in some places, large rocks in others. Attempts were made to level the rocks but the footing can be hazardous, especially if the rocks are wet, so go slowly. The route swings around the aptly named Rough Point, where surf often sprays high after crashing onto the boulders below. At times, the trail dips low, passing just above the waves, and then climbs again. At one point you'll find yourself beside a high chain-link fence topped by barbed wire with a relatively steep drop-off on the other side. In this area you cross a chasm on a wooden bridge; there is another ¼ mile or so of rough footing before the path goes up and follows the edge of a fenced lawn. This area provides excellent views of several more huge homes.

When the trail breaks out onto a street, you will be facing the last mansion on the route, Land's End, once the George Eustis Paine estate. The street is Ledge Road, and you turn to the right here whether you left a car on Ledge Road or plan to walk Bellevue Avenue back to Easton Beach. When you reach the top of Ledge Road, turn right and take Bellevue all the way back to Memorial Boulevard. The return is about 3 miles, most of it along what was once the most prestigious residential street in New England.

Beavertail Park

A scenic island walk through military and sailing history

Hiking distance: 3 miles
Hiking time: 2 hours
Difficulty: Relatively easy; some rock hopping in the early going, a narrow path along cliffs on the return walk, but alternatives are available

A walk in Beavertail State Park can be fascinating at any time of year. And you don't have to wait for good weather. In fact, in many ways it is more exciting, more inspiring, in stormy weather.

Beavertail is located at the southern tip of Jamestown Island in Narragansett Bay. There are no marked hiking trails through the park, but none is needed. A most interesting walk of about 3 miles can be made by following the rocky shoreline and cutting across the center of the park while checking out numerous bits of sailing and military history, as well as viewing waterfowl, songbirds, and other wildlife. You start and end at a picturesque lighthouse and can add visits to a small museum and aquarium, if desired.

Just below the lighthouse area are thousands of rocks of all sizes, and this is a good place to begin and end your visit. Once, Beavertail was among the most notorious places in New England for sailors. Shipwrecks dot its history—more than 30 vessels have been destroyed or have run aground here in the past 200 years—and when the waves are high and crashing into rocks below, it's easy to imagine how treacherous this place can be in a storm. In fact, you can still find a bit of cargo from a ship that went down in 1859.

In calmer weather, this is a place of beauty. Photographers and artists often can be found near the lighthouse, recording the white spray of the surf gleaming in the sunshine. Other visitors fish, picnic, sunbathe, or simply sit on the rocks and drink in the scenery.

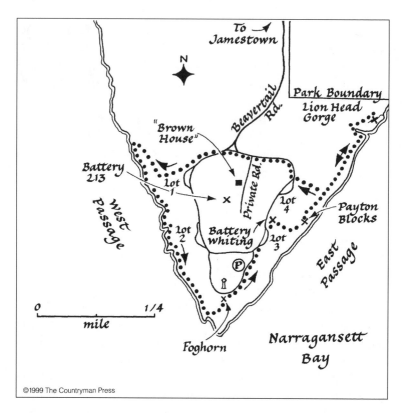

©1999 The Countryman Press

Access

Reaching the park is not difficult; only one road—Beavertail Road—runs due south out of the village of Jamestown. Follow it into the park, continue past the first two parking lots, swing around the lighthouse, and, if possible, park along the fence just beyond the buildings. If those spots are filled, as is often the case, continue to Lot 3 on the right.

Trail

Before walking, take a moment to look over signs just to the right of the roadway. One depicts the types of boats you're likely to see off Beavertail, and the other notes some of the sea life found at the water's edge. These bits of information can help you enjoy your visit to the park.

Begin by heading left (east) and checking out a tangle of bushes at the far edge of Lot 3. Hidden in this thicket is Battery Whiting, one of the bunkers established on Beavertail when it was known as Fort Burnside during World War II. A narrow, overgrown path near the road leads to the bunker, now sealed from entry. Just beyond, also engulfed by bushes, is part of an observation station that can still be entered. The view, however, is now obscured by the surging bushes. Gun placements just outside the station guarded Narragansett Bay's East Passage.

When you are ready to walk the shore, return to the grassy area beside Lot 3, take one of the paths down to the rocks, and turn left. For much of this section, you can follow the open grassland above the rocks, but you have to get closer to the water to see another of the park's features. Lying among the rocks at the water's edge (sometimes submerged when the tide is in) are large, rectangular granite blocks; these were destined for Alexandria, Virginia, aboard the *H.F. Payton* when it sank near here in 1859. The building blocks rested beneath the waves for nearly 80 years until the Hurricane of 1938 flung about a dozen of them onto the island. On close inspection, you can still see some of the flowery designs chiseled into the granite.

Throughout this area there are good views, looking back, of the lighthouse, and across the water to your left, of the city of Newport. Many seabirds frequent the offshore waters as well—terns, cormorants, and gulls in summer; scoters, eiders, and mergansers in winter.

Continue following the rocks. You'll notice numerous white streaks in them, showing different forms of stone, and then you'll reach an area where the rocks have a distinctly darker color, nearly black. As you proceed, take note of a concrete retaining wall just above the rocks; you'll need this for a landmark on your return trip. (If you are walking on the grassy upper path, the retaining wall is below another parking area, designated Lot 4. Only a terribly overgrown path continues into bushes beyond the lot, so you should go down onto the rocks here.) I recommend continuing on the rocks until the shore begins curving left. Here, if you're standing near the water, you can see both the lighthouse and Newport Bridge from one

Spraying surf and the lighthouse bring people to Beavertail time after time.

spot. And just below you is a deep chasm that cannot be crossed without going up into the bushes. This is Lion Head Gorge; when the waves rush into the cleft, the result is often a loud, booming crash that reminded an early visitor of a lion's roar. It's a good spot to linger and listen.

The path around the chasm goes on, but you would soon leave state property, so when you are ready to resume walking, return along the rocky shore, toward the lighthouse, until you reach the concrete headwall. Take one of the paths around the wall and you'll find Lot 4. Turn right onto the paved park road and follow it as it circles inland. Bushes line the road and often they are filled with small birds, particularly during spring and fall migrations. I've also seen a coyote trotting on this road, and more than once I've seen deer step from the dense thickets.

On your left, beyond the bushes, you can see part of a brown building with high radio antennae. This was a special wartime structure built as an identification and communications center to monitor all vessels in the bay. Great pains were taken to make the building resemble a summer cottage, but the walls are 3 feet thick, some of the "windows" are merely painted decorations, and the real windows were equipped with metal shields. The building is still in use and off-limits to visitors. Between the "brown house" and the lighthouse is another battery swallowed in thickets, an underground complex that is sometimes included in tours conducted by park rangers in summer. Visitors should not try to explore it on their own because the darkness and holes in the floors make wandering around extremely dangerous.

Stay on the paved road as it loops through the park interior. Pass the exit road on your right (the gravel lane going to your left leads to the brown building) and cross the road on which you entered. Go into a parking lot (Lot 1) on the right and look for a path leading off from the far right corner. This path will lead to some of the most difficult walking of the park, so if scrambling at a cliff's edge is not your idea of fun, remain on the paved road to Lot 2, where you can walk above the water in ease. The path from Lot 1 quickly forks; go left. In less than ¼ mile you'll find yourself at the top of a cliff above the water. An even narrower path runs along the rim to the left. For the next ½ mile, as you head back toward the lighthouse, you have the choice of either making like a mountain goat and clinging to the rocky slope or pushing through the bushes on the parallel path. Usually, a combination of the two is necessary both to enjoy the experience and the views and to circle several chasms.

This side of Beavertail usually is more sheltered than the southern and eastern exposures, particularly in winter, and as such is a favorite place for birders, many of whom use the parking lots above. During stormy weather, flocks of brant, scaup, and other wintering ducks and geese rest on this side, seeking refuge below these cliffs. In summer, sandpipers feed among the rocks, and there are always terns soaring by. The bushes above can usually be counted on for songbirds, while hawks of several species patrol the area.

After about ¼ mile of challenging scrambling, the lighthouse comes into view and walking gets much easier, although you still have to swing inland around some deep clefts. You can walk out onto the rocks and look over barnacles and other marine life found there, and perhaps feel the salt spray. Chances are, as you near the lighthouse, many other people will be doing the same.

As you make the half circle around the lighthouse, you'll see a large modern foghorn, and beside it part of the stonework of Beavertail's first lighthouse, built in 1749, the third to be established on the Atlantic coast. Your car is just ahead. Before leaving, though, visit the aquarium and the museum (open in warm-weather months and on weekends in winter), or pause and take another look at the timeless ocean. It hasn't changed in all these years, yet it is never exactly the same no matter how many times you see it.

Block Island South

A visit to the famous Mohegan Bluffs, other scenic highlights at the southern end of Block Island, and the quiet, forgotten center

Hiking distance: 9½ miles
Hiking time: 4–4½ hours
Difficulty: Easy but long; can be tedious because of extended stretches on pavement

If you are looking for something unique in your walks, take a trip to Block Island. There you can walk for many miles and continue to see sights not available anywhere else in Rhode Island.

Block Island, 12 miles south of the mainland, was once a farming and fishing community. Later it became something of a resort and vacation spot, earning the nickname Bermuda of the North. The beaches and shops and restaurants still draw crowds in summer, but in autumn—the best time to visit the island—the place is a quieter wonderland of seascapes, cliffs, plant life, bird life, and history.

The walk described here—9½ miles through the central and southeastern regions of the island—is one of the most popular routes, although far more visitors use mopeds and bicycles than their feet. Except for a detour through a spot appropriately called the Greenway in the center of the island, and another through an intriguing place known as Rodman's Hollow, the distance is easily enough traveled on wheels, but I wonder if even mopeds and bicycles are too fast; their riders may miss too much.

Access

As with the other Block Island hike (Walk 39), this one begins and ends in the village of New Shoreham at Old Harbor, where the ferryboats from Point Judith and Providence drop off and pick up passengers.

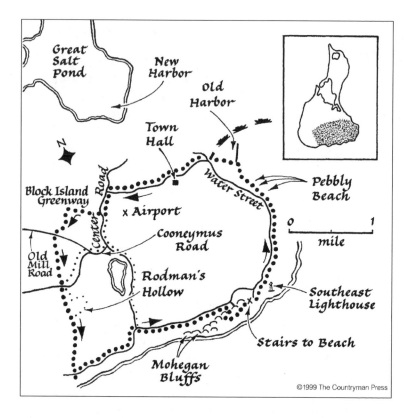

©1999 The Countryman Press

The walk can take 4 hours or considerably longer, if you do extra exploring or linger along Mohegan Bluffs, so it may be best to take the Point Judith ferry, which takes only an hour to reach the island. The trip from Providence is much longer and might not give you enough time to walk this loop and still catch a return ferry the same day.

Schedules vary with the seasons, so check departure times in advance.

Trail

From the landing, turn right onto the first street (Water Street) and then almost immediately go left onto Chapel Street, between the Harborside Inn and the New Shoreham House, two of the large wooden hotels built for tourists. Quickly, you leave the shops behind and start uphill, into a residential area. Chapel Street soon merges with Old Town Road, and in minutes you reach the town hall and the island's interior.

If you are used to forest walks, you will be struck by the absence of tall trees. Early settlers cut the trees in carving out their farms, and the ocean winds that buffet the island, frequently merciless in winter, prevent new vegetation from gaining much height. Still, there is much greenery all around. Fruit trees (apples, pears, peaches) line the first section of Old Town Road, and many are now being engulfed by swarming grapevines. Bayberry bushes, blackberry and honeysuckle vines, sumacs, and wild roses form thickets—virtually impenetrable walls—along the roadway. In summer and early fall, wildflowers are common and colorful.

When you reach Center Road, about 1 mile from your start and marked by millstones set in the ground, turn left and climb a rather steep hill. The road swings to the right around the island airport. On the opposite side of the road, to your right, you have an open view across lowlands to houses perched on hilltops along the western edge of the island.

As you begin to pass the airport, look on the right side of the road for the entrance to the Block Island Greenway, a walkers-only oasis in the center of the island. You could continue walking paved roads all the way to Rodman's Hollow, but taking a detour is a most pleasant respite from walking on pavement and enables you to experience a part of Block Island that few visitors even know exists. The Greenway offers open, grassy lanes, plenty of bird life, wildflowers and blossoming bushes in summer, and a good chance to see deer. Many miles of trails wander through the Greenway, and you could spend most of a day exploring it, but to leave time for reaching the island's south coast, this walk takes a fairly direct route through the Greenway and then follows a lane called the Greenway Link to Rodman's Hollow. (For more on the features of the Greenway, see Walk 21, *More Walks and Rambles in Rhode Island,* Backcountry Publications.)

Before venturing into the Greenway, take a moment to look over the kiosk, which often provides information on the birds and

Mohegan Bluffs tower above the ocean on Block Island's south side.

plants you may encounter. If you are visiting in summer, you are likely to find the trail flanked by fragrant wild roses, honeysuckles, and other flowering bushes and vines. After about ⅓ mile, you reach a pine-covered slope, and halfway up the slope you reach a fork. Go left; a sign indicates that it is the route to the Turnip Farm. Continue following signs for Turnip Farm until you emerge from the small woodlot. Now you are at another fork, facing an open meadow that once was part of the farm. Go left, keeping the meadow on your right and a house on the left. Ahead you should see a fenced enclosure. It appears to be an animal pen but is actually a means of keeping deer from eating the northern blazing star, an endangered wildflower that blooms in August.

Just beyond the high fence, a path breaks to the right, and straight ahead is a parking lot on a gravel road called Old Mill Road. If you wish to save yourself some steps and possibly some confusion, go out onto the gravel road, turn right, and walk less than ¹⁄₁₀ mile until you reach another Greenway exit on your right and wooden stairs over a stone wall on your left. This ladder is the entrance to the Greenway Link.

However, if you want to see more of the Greenway, take the right fork at the fence. Numerous side paths run off this lane, so *remain on the wide, mowed trail as it winds uphill.* After going up the short but steep slope, take all lefts. In moments you should see an old plank bridge over a small brook. This path will take you past a house and out to Old Mill Road and the wooden stairway. The Greenway Link is merely a ¼-mile shortcut through a pretty area of meadows, bushes, and stone walls to Cooneymus Road and the beginning of Rodman's Hollow. The link is across private property, so be sure to remain on the lane.

After crossing Cooneymus Road, the Greenway trail angles left to a wonderful old dirt lane, Black Rock Road, that skirts the edge of Rodman's Hollow, one of the island's natural highlights. The deep hollow is supposedly the favorite haunt of the Block Island meadow vole, a mouselike animal found nowhere else on earth. Hawks that feed on the vole and other small prey also are common in the hollow, along with numerous songbirds, especially during migration seasons.

Black Rock Road, one of my favorite walking places on the entire island, runs for about 1 mile to the south shore. It also provides access to some of the better trails going into the hollow. From this lane, rocky and rutted in places, you can usually see hawks soaring, hear pheasants crowing, and often see deer or, at the very least, deer tracks. The view to the right, opposite the hollow, is of rolling hills sectioned off by stone walls.

Immediately upon reaching Black Rock Road, you'll pass a turnstile on the left and a trail leading into the hollow. Take this path for a closer look at the plants, birds, and butterflies. Since the trails in the hollow wander erratically, take *all right turns.* When you pass benches installed on a hillside, look for a narrow side path to the right. It will lead you back out to Black Rock Road.

By now you can see the ocean ahead, and as you near the shoreline, you will reach a junction with another dirt road, running left. This will be your way back to pavement, but first go a few yards straight ahead to the cliff above Black Rock Beach. You can pause here and enjoy the sounds and sights of the surf far below, or you can take a path down to the water. This is roughly the halfway point in your walk, and a delightful place for a rest.

When you are ready to resume, return to the dirt road you passed just before the bluff. It is now on your right. This is a fairly long walk past several homes and some impressive overlooks before you reach pavement. Turn right onto the paved road, Mohegan Trail, which runs to the island's most famous cliffs.

The bluffs were named for the Mohegan war party that was driven over these cliffs by the island's Native Americans, the Manisseans, in 1590. The highest bluffs tower 200 feet above the beach and ocean, and you can reach these cliffs by two chief cutoffs.

I like to take the first side trail, an unmarked sandy lane that runs through the dunes from a point where the paved road jogs left. The lane runs to the edge of a cliff that provides spectacular views of bluffs on both sides as well as of the Southeast Lighthouse in the distance on the left.

From this cliff, you can take a rather steep path to the right down to the beach. Be careful; it's a little treacherous. (If the climb down the cliff does not appeal to you, simply return to the paved road and walk to the next dirt lane and a sign for the Payne Overlook.) Once on the beach, turn left and walk the few hundred yards to a wooden stairway. The 160 steps will take you back up the cliff to an observation platform. This spot is the most commonly used vista for both Mohegan Bluffs and Southeast Light and is likely to be crowded in summer.

When you return to the paved road, turn right. Ahead looms Southeast Light, which carries a beam that ships can see for 30 miles. Near the lighthouse, which was moved inland more than 150 feet in 1993 because of fears that it someday would fall victim to the eroding cliff, is a stone that lists the names of 16 ships that were wrecked along this shore, a list that ends with the chilling "etc."

You are now on Southeast Light Road, heading back toward the village, and if you visit in summer, you are likely to be dodging mopeds and bicycles. The road name is soon changed to Spring Street. Where the road runs near the water, you may want to leave the pavement one last time. You can cross the guardrail and take a path down the aptly named Pebbly Beach. It's just a short walk on this beach to a restaurant, an excellent place to refresh yourself while awaiting your ferry back to the mainland.

Block Island North

A look at the quieter end of historic Block Island: ocean scenes, a picturesque lighthouse, and rare birds

Hiking distance: 10 miles
Hiking time: 4–4½ hours
Difficulty: Long but easy, except for some hilly areas along Clay Head

The northern end of Block Island offers the walker a wide variety of sights: a flotilla of boats and a lovely, quiet pond; a sand-dune wildlife sanctuary and a dense, junglelike thicket; a low-lying spit of land and high, rugged cliffs; and a postcard-perfect old lighthouse that looks the way lighthouses should look.

This walk also offers less crowded areas than most of the island, which attracts increasingly large numbers of vacationers and day-trippers in summer. It is a long walk, about 10 miles—more if you spend much time rambling in a thicket called The Maze, exploring the cliffs at Clay Head, or wandering about the famed North Light—but it is an easy stroll, with much of the route on one paved road. The only slightly strenuous areas are sections of the cliff trail at Clay Head.

Because of the distance and the fact that so much of the route is on that one road, an alternative might be to bicycle to the beginning of the Clay Head Trail, and then start your walking. That would leave you far more time for enjoying the attractions at the island's north end, particularly if you are spending only the day on the island and must return in time to catch a mainland-bound ferry. I nearly always include a bike in my visits to the north end.

Access

As with the Block Island South hike (Walk 38), this route begins and ends at the ferry landing at Old Harbor in New Shoreham. Ferry schedules vary with the season, and sometimes change within a sea-

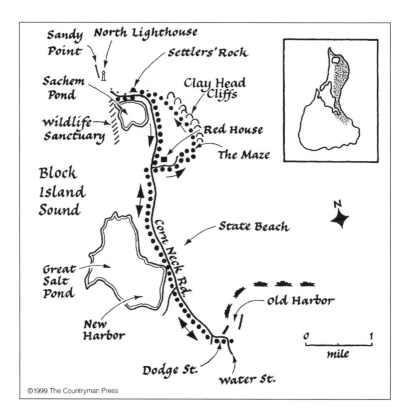

son, so check departure times from Point Judith and for the return trip in advance.

Trail

From the landing at Old Harbor, go right onto Water Street, past the souvenir shops and the large wooden hotels that were built when New Shoreham was the "Bermuda of the North" around 1900. Turn left onto Dodge Street, then take the first right onto Corn Neck Road and you're all set. Corn Neck Road runs all the way to the northern tip of the island.

You could also walk the beach in this section, but this is a long walk, and the sand may make you too weary too soon. The road is easier, even though you may have to contend with cars, mopeds, and bicycles headed for the state beach, just ahead, or going to New Harbor.

Shortly after leaving the village, you will begin seeing, past houses on the left, a small pond and then the masts of sailboats moored in Great Salt Pond; but before reaching the pond itself you will pass, on the right, the parking lot and pavilion for the state beach, always crowded in summer. Once past the beach entrance, you get your best views of the large pond, New Harbor, often filled with boats. A wooden walkway enables you to get to the pond's shore, and sailing enthusiasts will enjoy the panoramic view of the flotilla of watercraft.

Past the pond, the road runs between old farms and a steadily increasing number of new houses and cottages. For the most part this section is uneventful, but it can be surprising; on one walk here I found a yellow-headed blackbird, a species rare in New England. Rare birds are among the reasons many people come to Block Island, particularly in fall. Many migratory birds use the island as a resting place, and seabirds that seldom appear on the mainland seek refuge here during storms. The increase in birds, as well as the decrease in crowds and traffic, makes autumn the ideal time to walk the island.

Just over 3 miles from your start is a sandy side road that runs to the ocean and The Maze, a privately owned thicket in which the owners have cut numerous narrow, winding trails. Take this sandy road, identified by a signpost that says CLAY HEAD TRAIL. If you are biking, you can ride ½ mile on this road, but then you will have to leave the bike and walk the final ¼ mile to the bluffs and The Maze. If you so desire, you can spend an entire day wandering these trails and the nearby cliffs, but if you also want to reach a monument known as Settlers' Rock and the lighthouse beyond, it might be best simply to spend a few moments admiring the rocky shore, then follow the trail that runs up to the top of the cliffs. You'll quickly pass a sign that says PRIVATE PROPERTY, WALKERS WELCOME; this is the beginning of The Maze, an intricate network of paths created and maintained by the Lapham family. Throughout the next 1¼ miles, you'll be passing numerous paths going to the left into thickets of trees and bushes. If you wish to wander a few of the paths, you are likely to see and hear dozens of songbirds and perhaps spot a deer or two.

At first, the trail toward the top of the cliffs is disappointing,

North Light is among the famous landmarks on Block Island.

because dense bushes offer few open views of the sea, but there are good vistas ahead, and they are spectacular indeed. If you are visiting in summer, you will find yourself looking down on scores of bank swallows swooping over the beach area. The swallows nest in the face of the cliffs, as do a few barn owls, a bird extremely rare in Rhode Island.

In addition to the sea views and the dense brush, you will pass two idyllic little ponds. When you begin seeing houses, you are nearing Corn Neck Road, and you finish this trail by walking a sandy road that leads to houses. You emerge directly across from Sachem Pond, a picturesque pond that, along with the rugged dunes on the opposite shore, makes up a wildlife refuge. The dunes are the nesting site of numerous gulls, terns, and other birds.

Corn Neck Road, going to the right, ends at Settlers' Rock, the monument that commemorates the arrival, in 1661, of the 16 Boston men who became the first permanent white inhabitants of the island. Near the rock, which is about 5 miles from your start, are picnic tables and a small beach, making it an excellent place to rest.

The ambitious can continue, however, as a pebble-strewn beach runs farther out on the point, to North Light, the grand old landmark saved from demolition a few years ago. Now the much photographed lighthouse, built in 1867 (the fourth lighthouse on this site), is open as an interpretive center in summer. Beyond the light is Sandy Point, a narrow, sometimes submerged sandbar that has been the scene of a great many shipwrecks over the centuries.

So there is plenty to do and see at the north end. However, sooner or later you will have to leave this alluring place and head back toward the ferry. You can return via the Clay Head Trail, the best bet if you came by bicycle, or by walking Corn Neck Road all the way back. The road back includes a rather steep climb, but at the top of the hill, on a clear day, you may be able to see Gardiners Island and Fishers Island, part of New York State, as well as some of the Connecticut shoreline, mainland Rhode Island, and a bit of the Massachusetts shore—four states from one vantage point.

Remember, though, that from Settlers' Rock it is more than 4 miles along the paved road back to the ferry. Make sure you give yourself enough time. The one thing you don't want to do on Block Island is hurry.

North South Trail

40

At last, a chance to walk the length of Rhode Island, from the ocean to the Massachusetts line

Hiking distance: 77 miles
Difficulty: Mostly easy, with a few short sections of rocky
footing. The most challenging aspect is the length.

It took more than 20 years between the planning and fruition, but walkers can now traverse Rhode Island, following blue blazes from the ocean beach in Charlestown to the Massachusetts line in Burrillville. This trail links seven state management areas on the western edge of Rhode Island (Burlingame, Carolina, Arcadia, Nicholas Farm, Durfee Hill, George Washington, and Buck Hill) and enables walkers to explore beautiful and diverse properties.

No estimated hiking time is given for this trail, because nobody is likely to walk it in one stretch. Because the trail is so long, and done in increments, it is not possible to provide as many details as on the other walks in this book, nor suggested parking places except for those finishing up at Buck Hill in Burrillville. Those who tackle this trail will decide for themselves how much they can handle in a day or weekend. There are few legal camping places along the trail, but several commercial campgrounds lie within a couple of miles of the route, particularly in the southern half.

Between the management areas, the trail does emerge on roads several times, once for more than 10 miles and for more than 8 miles in another segment. If there is a drawback to this magnificent project, it is the number of miles on roads. Every effort was made to stay off roads, and when no alternative could be found, the trail designers chose scenic, little-traveled back roads as often as possible. Still, I find myself using a bicycle on the longer road stretches.

The route described here, which includes a detour into Connecticut, may not be the final version. A section in Glocester may yet be rerouted to avoid going into Connecticut and to eliminate some of

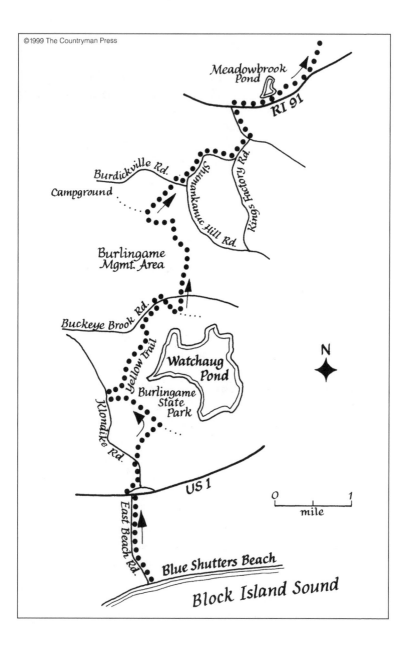

Meadowbrook
Pond

RI 91

Burdickville Rd.

Kings Factory Rd.

Shumankanuc Hill Rd.

Campground

Burlingame
Mgmt. Area

Buckeye Brook Rd.

Yellow Trail

Watchaug
Pond

Burlingame
State
Park

Klondike Rd.

N

US 1

0   1
mile

East Beach Rd.

Blue Shutters Beach

Block Island Sound

the miles on roads.

The North South was designed as a multiuse trail but in some places, such as where it crosses areas susceptible to erosion or other damage, there are HIKERS ONLY signs. In these areas, other paths are designated for horseback riders and bicyclists.

Much of the trail follows other hiking paths already detailed in this book and in the companion guide, *More Walks and Rambles in Rhode Island* (Backcountry Publications). Also, more detailed information is available from the North South Trail Council, which holds Treks each spring that cover the entire trail in several weekends. Contact Ginny Leslie at 401-781-8117 for more information.

Access

To begin at the southern terminus, take US 1 to East Beach Road in Charlestown, turn south onto East Beach, and drive to the ocean. The trail's official start is at Blue Shutters Beach, where East Beach Road reaches the ocean.

Trail

The first segment is a walk back up East Beach Road, past homes, to and across busy US 1, a distance of about 1¼ miles. After crossing the highway, the trail goes right onto Old 1A briefly, then left onto Klondike Road. After nearly ½ mile on Klondike, you get your first chance for woods walking when the trail turns right into Burlingame State Park. In another ¾ mile, the North South Trail (NST) joins the yellow-blazed Vin Gormley Trail (Walk 3) and follows that path for the next 4 miles. This segment runs on some wooden walkways, crosses brooks, and, after emerging onto Buckeye Brook Road and then returning to forest, wanders along some interesting rock outcroppings. The NST leaves the yellow Gormley Trail blazes atop a flat table rock and turns left, going out to Buckeye Brook Road. The road is approximately 6¼ miles from your start at the beach.

By crossing Buckeye Brook Road, the trail enters Burlingame State Management Area. For about the next 1½ miles, the NST runs with Burlingame North (Walk 4) on an old woods road called Clawson

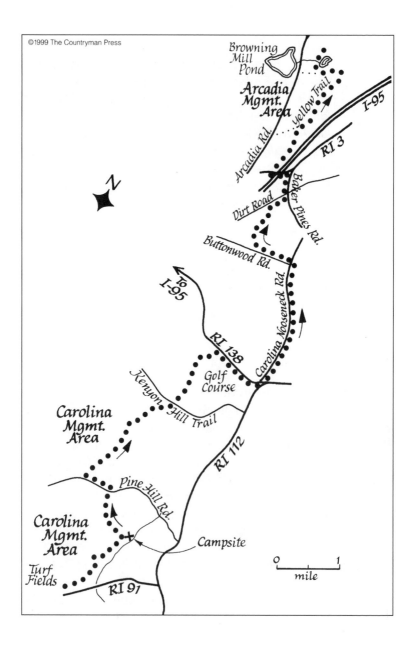

Browning
Mill
Pond

Arcadia
Mgmt.
Area

Yellow Trail

I-95

Arcadia Rd.

RI 3

Dirt Road

Baker Pines Rd.

N

Buttonwood Rd.

To
I-95

Carolina Nooseneck Rd.

RI 138

Golf
Course

Kenyon Hill Trail

RI 112

Carolina
Mgmt.
Area

Pine Hill Rd.

Carolina
Mgmt.
Area

Campsite

Turf
Fields

RI 91

0   1
mile

Trail, through an attractive forest that features stone dams and brooks. At a T-intersection, Burlingame North goes left (and swings down to a campground on the Pawcatuck River) while the blue NST turns right. It continues in woods for less than 1 mile before emerging on paved Burdickville Road. You'll be on roads for the next 3⅓ miles. Turn right onto Burdickville, then left onto Shumankanuc Road, and left again onto Kings Factory Road. These roads, too, are paved but are pleasant enough, with farms and homes, a crossing over the Pawcatuck River and a railroad track, and not particularly heavy traffic. After more than 2 miles on these three roads, however, you reach RI 91, a considerably busier highway. Turn right onto RI 91 and continue more than ½ mile, passing through Wood River Junction to the Meadow Brook Pond Fishing Area on the left side of the highway. This spot, about 11¾ miles from your start, is where many NST hikers conclude their first day's effort.

From the fishing area, the trail follows dirt roads, first through a wooded area and then along the right edge of a large farm field usually growing turf. When the farm lane reaches a red barn, it turns left and goes through the field, past a shed, and finally curves left to a dilapidated barn, where in summer you are likely to encounter numerous barn swallows. The trail curls around the barn, follows the edge of woods to the right, and then enters the Carolina Management Area on a woods lane. From this point until the NST emerges on Pine Hill Road, you are on the Carolina South Trail (Walk 8), walking through a quiet pine forest. There is a campsite in this area, on the banks of the Pawcatuck River. After leaving the river, the trail runs beside a cemetery and past cellar holes through another grove of impressive pines before reaching Pine Hill Road.

Once you are on the road, turn left and follow the blue blazes past the official entrance to Carolina (you can find an outhouse here) and down the road until you cross a bridge. Here, the NST forks, a multiuse section going to the right down a gravel lane and a hikers-only route remaining on the road a few yards more before entering the woods on a narrow path. Descriptions of both forks are included in the Carolina North Trail (Walk 9).

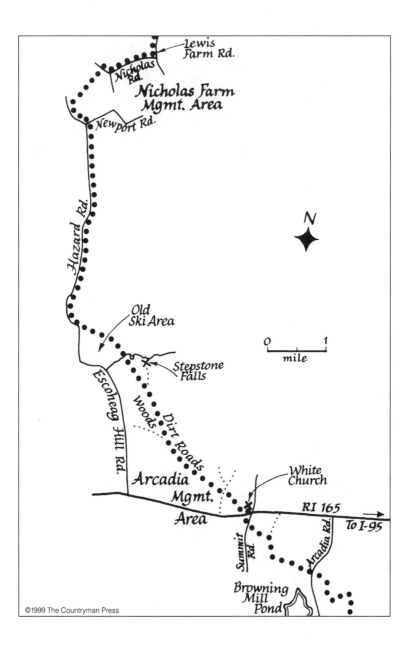

The blue trails rejoin before leaving this picturesque area of old roads, mixed forest, and rock outcroppings. The NST then follows a lane out of the woods, past several houses, to and across a paved road (Kenyon Hill Trail), before returning to forest on a most pleasant lane that features immense outcroppings on the left. I've seen deer in this section and mother grouse going through their broken-wing acts, which indicate that eggs or babies are probably nearby.

You emerge from this woods beside a golf course on the left, and the trail goes through a residential development briefly. Be careful to watch the blue blazes; they make an abrupt right onto a dead-end street called Wildwood Court. After another short segment through a damp woods, the trail emerges onto RI 138, a busy highway, behind a gas station where you can get a cold drink if so inclined. From here, you will be on roads for 3-plus miles. First turning to the right on RI 138, you immediately pass a golf course and then follow the highway around a curve to the left, passing Richmond Elementary School and then turning left onto scenic but hilly Carolina-Nooseneck Road. After another left onto Buttonwood Road, the trail returns to the woods on the right, entering the state's largest management area, Arcadia.

The first mile in Arcadia is hilly and rocky. Be careful not to wander off on unmarked side paths. The blue blazes lead to a power-line strip (turn right) and then out to a paved road, Baker Pines Road. Go left, and you quickly reach RI 3, which runs parallel to I-95. Go left onto RI 3, but stay on it only long enough to pass under the interstate. Then immediately go right onto a gravel lane. When the gravel lane turns left, the blue blazes go straight ahead in the woods, returning to the Arcadia Management Area. Now you can forget about cars and traffic for several miles.

Soon, you join up with a yellow-blazed path, the Arcadia Trail (Walk 22). Turn right and you are in for a delightful stretch or a maddening one, depending on your opinion of boulder fields and rocky brooks. There are a couple of places where the blue trail splits off from the yellow briefly, but they rejoin and you are following Arcadia for several miles, visiting a forgotten chimney and several attractive woods lanes. When very close to the Arcadia Trail's end at RI 165, the NST breaks off to the left and follows a lane through a pine grove to a gravel road called Summit Road.

This road is the beginning of the Mount Tom Trail (Walk 20). Instead of going left, as Mount Tom's white blazes do, turn right, cross the highway to a white church, and follow the blue blazes as they angle to the left down a woods lane. You are now walking, in reverse direction, the final leg of Walk 20, crossing a couple of popular fishing rivers and going up a dirt road called Barber Trail. This is a most pleasant section with some open fields and often provides glimpses of deer and birds among the flowers.

Pay attention to the blazes; they turn off the road after about 1 mile from the Barber Trail signpost amid the stone walls and foundations of what was a farm site, going to the right through what is left of an orchard. The trail now becomes a bit hilly and curvy before reaching a flatter stretch and joining the white-blazed Escoheag Trail (Walk 16) coming in from the left. Together, the trails soon emerge on a dirt road, where the Escoheag terminates.

The blue trail crosses this dirt road and returns to the woods on a fire lane, but here I recommend leaving the NST for a while. Go to the right the few yards to a river and follow a yellow-blazed path called the Ben Utter Trail (Walk 19). This trail follows the hurrying little Falls River and is a far more picturesque walk than is the woods lane. As suggested in Walk 19, when you see a white trail angling downhill from the yellow path, take it to the right for the best views of Stepstone Falls, a truly lovely spot. The blue trail eventually emerges just above the falls onto a dirt road, but it misses some of the most scenic places in this area.

After reaching this dirt road, the NST goes to the left on the road a short distance, then returns to the forest on the right on a hikers-only path. Bikers and horse riders must remain on the road out to Escoheag Hill Road and then turn right. Walkers will cut through a damp, often muddy segment—the reason for barring wheels and horses—and then stroll through the former Pine Top Ski Area (Walk 40, *More Walks and Rambles in Rhode Island,* Backcountry Publications).

Farm scenes make the road segments of NST easier to take.

After emerging from woods, you'll see the old ski slopes on your left before crossing an open area and reaching a barway beside a road where pavement yields way to gravel. This is Hazard Road, which you follow for the next 4 miles.

Going to the right on the gravel road, you pass several farms, a couple of picturesque ponds, and plenty of woods as you cross from West Greenwich into Coventry. The road, which becomes paved for a while, then switches back to gravel, is lightly traveled, relatively flat, and runs through woods after the first couple of miles. It can be as pleasant as most woods hikes, and about as wild. Once, in this stretch, a hawk flew by, just inches from my face, carrying a chipmunk.

When you reach a T-intersection at another gravel road, Newport Road, you are approaching the Nicholas Farm Management Area. The trail goes to the left on Newport Road for about ⅓ mile, then enters the woods on the right just before the Connecticut line. This woods segment of about 1 mile is easy and pleasant but unspectacular with second-growth trees. The trail emerges onto a dirt lane, Nicholas Road, and you return to road walking for the next 1⅓ miles.

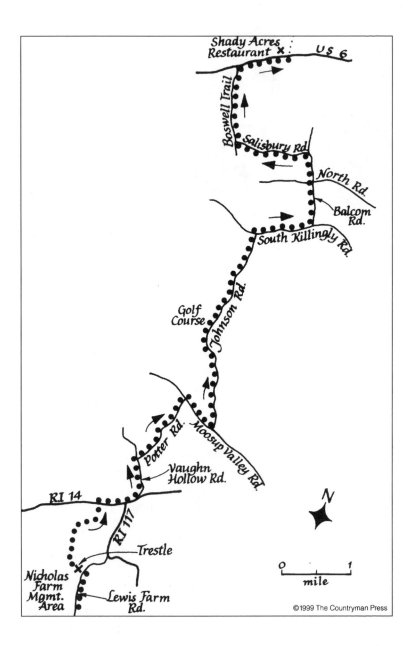

Shady Acres
Restaurant ✗
US 6

Boswell Trail

Salisbury Rd.

North Rd.

Balcom
Rd.

South Killingly Rd.

Golf
Course

Johnson Rd.

Potter Rd.

Moosup Valley Rd.

Vaughn
Hollow Rd.

RI 14

RI 117

Trestle

Nicholas
Farm
Mgmt.
Area

Lewis Farm
Rd.

N

0   1
mile

©1999 The Countryman Press

Shortly after turning right onto Nicholas Road, you'll reach another dirt road going to the right; it leads to a beaver pond that spills over the road, and those who like wildlife may find the 1-mile detour worthwhile. The blue blazes remain on Nicholas Road as it passes a large old barn foundation and the management area's parking lot, crosses a stream, passes a few houses, then ends at Lewis Farm Road. Turn left onto Lewis Farm Road, also a dirt road, and go about ⅓ mile, passing several more houses, until you reach a lane going to the left. This is a former railroad bed and leads to a trestle high above the Moosup River, a great place to linger. Much of the rest of the NST's stay in the Nicholas Farm Management Area is described in Walk 39 of *More Walks and Rambles in Rhode Island* (Backcountry Publications).

A few hundred yards beyond the trestle, the trail turns to the right and enters a pine forest. It follows a wide, easy lane until it makes an abrupt right in a small clearing and drops down a steep slope. The trail then follows the river a short distance to Spencer's Rock, an idyllic little waterfall that also is likely to make you linger. From the river, the trail cuts through a pine grove, crosses an open hay field, then turns left and wanders through a most impressive stand of tall pines before reaching RI 14. Enjoy the soft footing of pine needles; once you emerge onto RI 14, you are in for your longest stretch of road walking—more than 10 miles—on the entire NST.

Still, the roads are quite attractive and this can be a pleasant stretch, although probably better suited for biking than hiking. When you reach RI 14, go right (east), cross the Moosup River bridge, then bear left at the intersection with RI 117. At the next junction, turn left onto Vaughn Hollow Road, a paved road that runs past the old Rice City church and one-room schoolhouse. After less than 1 mile on this road, turn right onto Potter Road, a gravel lane that runs past small horse farms and through woods areas before emerging onto Moosup Valley Road, a busier highway.

Go right onto Moosup Valley Road but continue for only ½ mile, then go left onto Johnson Road at a sign for the Foster Country

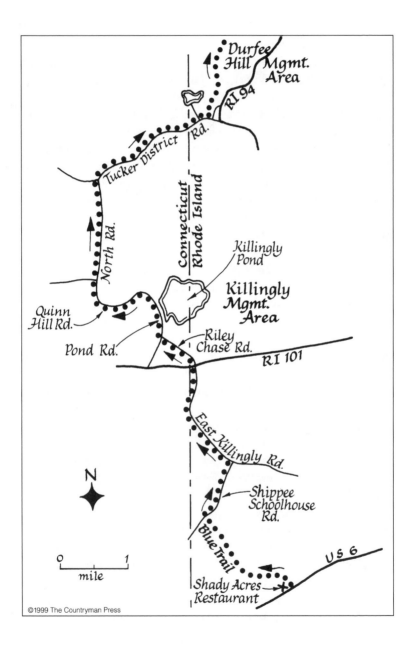

Durfee Hill Mgmt. Area

RI 94

Tucker District Rd.

Connecticut Rhode Island

North Rd.

Killingly Pond

Killingly Mgmt. Area

Quinn Hill Rd.

Pond Rd.

Riley Chase Rd.

RI 101

East Killingly Rd.

Shippee Schoolhouse Rd.

N

Blue Trail

US 6

Shady Acres Restaurant

0   1
mile

©1999 The Countryman Press

Club. You will be on Johnson Road for more than 3 miles, and while it is long and hilly, it is most attractive. In addition to the country club and golf course, you'll pass farms, open fields, Colonial homes, and thriving woodlands. Also, just down Harrington Road, which you reach in the center of the golf course, is a commercial campground for those seeking a place to stay for a night.

At the end of Johnson Road, go right onto South Killingly Road, passing another scenic horse farm, then take a left onto Balcom Road, a gravel road. As with most of these roads, Balcom is flanked by forests and horse farms. The surface turns to pavement and you cross North Road. Then take a left onto Salisbury, which has only a few homes, but they are large and impressive. At Boswell Trail, turn right. This is a pleasant stretch of homes featuring well-kept lawns, gardens, and stone walls. Boswell ends at US 6. The NST turns right, but you might want to go left a few yards to a gas station, where you can get a cold drink. You've earned it.

The NST goes right (east) onto US 6 less than ½ mile to the Shady Acres restaurant on the left side of the highway. Here, you finally return to the woods. Look for a lane entering the forest from the far right corner of a parking area just beyond the restaurant. Old maps show this lane as Tom Wood Road. You are in the woods for the next 1½ miles. There are forks in the trail, but the NST route is not hard to follow. At the first fork, you bear left, and at the second, you turn right. This section is straight and narrow, running along an old road now virtually engulfed in bushes. Eventually, you should notice stone walls on both sides, and where the road is badly eroded and you see steps in a wall on the right, you are nearing one of the highlights of this area. Just past the steps is a small pond on the right; on the left are the remains of a 19th-century shingle mill. The stonework, unique in design, is worth inspecting.

Shortly after passing the mill ruins, your trail breaks out of the woods onto a paved road, Shippee Schoolhouse Road. Turn right. In about 1 mile, passing mostly woods interspersed with homes, you reach a T-junction. Go left. This is East Killingly Road, and you follow it to its end at RI 101, just about on the Connecticut line.

The next segment is not blazed and may soon be changed; efforts are being made to secure passage through private property north of RI 101, allowing the NST to continue through the Killingly Management Area out to RI 94, and then possibly through the eastern side of the Durfee Hill Management Area and into the George Washington Management Area near a campground. As of this writing, however, the trail curls several miles around the Connecticut side of Killingly Pond on roads, so this might be another area best covered by bicycle.

The route used in recent years crosses RI 101 and goes down Riley Chase Road (directly across from East Killingly Road), right onto Pond Road, past Killingly Pond, then through hemlock groves up a steep slope called Quinn Hill. You continue straight at a stop sign, then take North Road as it curves to the right. This is a very scenic stretch with elaborate farms, homes, orchards, and panoramic views to the west. After a long downhill segment, turn right onto Tucker District Road and continue for a couple of miles, returning to Rhode Island on a gravel road.

The first left off this gravel road goes to a bridge and former mill site mentioned in the Durfee Hill hike (Walk 26). The NST route, however, continues straight ahead on the gravel road until it crosses a stream just before reaching RI 94. At the road junction, look for a narrow path angling back to the left across a small field. This is your entry into the Durfee Hill Management Area, a place with remarkable rock ledges and outcroppings. At present the route is not blazed, and the going can be extremely confusing because of the numerous paths, lanes, and logging roads. Until it is blazed, I suggest going with somebody who knows the way or joining one of the NST spring Treks. This stretch may not be included if the trail is rerouted through Glocester. NST veterans, by the way, call this 2-mile segment the Hemlock Ledges Trail, but it should not be confused with the trail (Walk 13) of the same name in the Arcadia Management Area.

The trail leaves the woods at US 44 and goes into Pulaski State Park. This leads to the final segment of the walk; it's about 12½ miles from the Pulaski parking lot to a lot in the Buck Hill Management

This quiet little pond lies hidden in the Buck Hill section of NST.

Area, so it might be a good idea to leave a car there. Parking is not available at the NST terminus itself at the Massachusetts line. To find the Buck Hill lot, follow the directions given for the Buck Hill Trail (Walk 28).

Pulaski Park also could be eliminated in rerouting, but for now the NST crosses US 44 and follows Pulaski Road into the park. Again, the NST is not blazed through the park, so care must be taken. Continue down the paved entrance road until you reach a parking area near a pond. Go along the left side of the pond, crossing on a bridge above a dam, then take a white-blazed path to the right along the shore. This is the reverse direction of the final leg of the Peck Pond Trail and the Pulaski Park Trail (Walks 1 and 2 in *More Walks and Rambles in Rhode Island,* Backcountry Publications).

In minutes, you reach a gravel woods road; turn right. This road, a popular cross-country ski trail in winter, is shaded with tall trees, many of them hemlocks, and features little stone-lined water holes built as protection against fire. After crossing an orange-blazed foot-

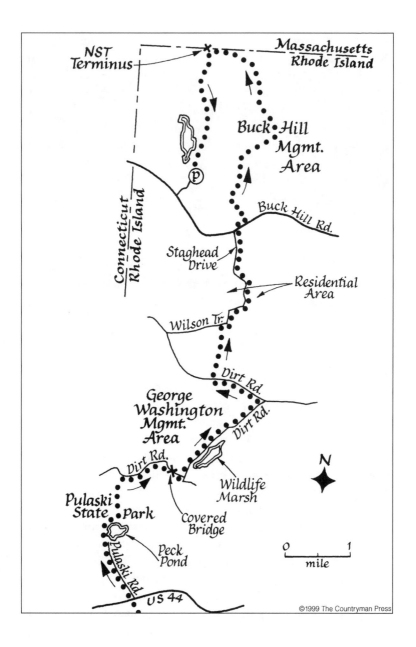

path, the Walkabout Trail (Walk 27), you reach a covered bridge and then a red gate and an intersection. Go left. On park maps, this gravel lane, which runs through much of the George Washington Management Area, is Richardson Trail, but there are no signposts in this area. In moments, you can see a marsh just to the right of the lane. A path to the marsh and its dam allows easy access and a place to linger. The marsh, built for wildlife, is detailed in the Walkabout Trail description. That trail crosses the earthen dam.

Back on the gravel lane (Richardson Trail is likely to be retained in any rerouting), you cross the Walkabout's orange blazes again, then meander through dense forest, the tallest trees now oaks and pines. The walking is relatively easy. After crossing a low ridge, the trail forks; go left. You are now on Monyan Trail and can begin looking for a hikers-only cutoff on the right. After you see the first square sign for the cutoff, go another 50 yards or so to the path itself, marked by two more small signs. This shortcut, less than 1 mile long, is hilly, rocky, and not worn, but it is blazed well. About halfway through, you reach an open gravel lane but return to forest directly across it. When you reach a narrower woods road, you are on Wilson Trail. Turn right.

In about ⅓ mile you leave the forest and enter a housing development. Take the first left, Staghead Drive, and follow it out through several turns, for just under 1 mile, to a highway, Buck Hill Road. Now you are ready for your final push to the Massachusetts state line. Go right (east) onto Buck Hill Road for less than ¼ mile. Across from pole 42, the trail returns to forest on the left. This 4-mile path is the longest section cut specifically for the NST. It's a very well-designed trail, done mostly by volunteer Bill Hendrickson, that winds and weaves through the rocky woods in order to reach the most interesting places. Features, in addition to numerous boulders and brooks, include a rock-edged pond and a high rock ledge.

You cross a gravel lane, and when the trail straightens out, you are on the state line heading west. At the next woods road you reach the official terminus of the NST, a stone marker indicating

Completing the entire North South Trail is quite an accomplishment.

the beginning of the Midstate Trail, which runs all the way across Massachusetts to New Hampshire. Take a moment to savor your accomplishment; you have walked the length of Rhode Island.

To reach the Buck Hill parking lot, turn left from the stone marker onto the woods road. You'll now find yellow blazes and can follow these blazes most of the way to the parking lot. In minutes after leaving the Midstate marker, you arrive at the deep-cut Old Starr Road, which is part of the Buck Hill Trail, and for the rest of this walk you are reversing the first part of the Walk 28 route. After passing a wildlife marsh, on your right, and the end of the yellow blazes, simply follow the gravel lane out to the parking lot. And then celebrate.

Let Backcountry Guides Take You There

Our experienced backcountry authors will lead you to the finest trails, parks, and back roads in the following areas:

50 Hikes Series

50 Hikes in the Adirondacks
50 Hikes in Connecticut
50 Hikes in the Maine Mountains
50 Hikes in Coastal and Southern Maine
50 Hikes in Massachusetts
50 Hikes in Maryland
50 Hikes in Michigan
50 Hikes in the White Mountains
50 More Hikes in New Hampshire
50 Hikes in New Jersey
50 Hikes in Central New York
50 Hikes in Western New York
50 Hikes in the Mountains of North Carolina
50 Hikes in Ohio
50 Hikes in Eastern Pennsylvania
50 Hikes in Central Pennsylvania
50 Hikes in Western Pennsylvania
50 Hikes in the Tennessee Mountains
50 Hikes in Vermont
50 Hikes in Northern Virginia

Walks and Rambles Series

Walks and Rambles on Cape Cod and the
   Islands
Walks and Rambles on the Delmarva Peninsula
Walks and Rambles in the Western
   Hudson Valley
Walks and Rambles on Long Island
Walks and Rambles in Ohio's Western Reserve
Walks and Rambles in Rhode Island
Walks and Rambles in and around St. Louis

25 Bicycle Tours Series

25 Bicycle Tours in the Adirondacks
25 Bicycle Tours on Delmarva
25 Bicycle Tours in Savannah and the Carolina
   Low Country
25 Bicycle Tours in Maine
25 Bicycle Tours in Maryland
25 Bicycle Tours in the Twin Cities and
   Southeastern Minnesota
30 Bicycle Tours in New Jersey
30 Bicycle Tours in the Finger Lakes Region
25 Bicycle Tours in the Hudson Valley
25 Bicycle Tours in Ohio's Western Reserve
25 Bicycle Tours in the Texas Hill Country and
   West Texas
25 Bicycle Tours in Vermont
25 Bicycle Tours in and around Washington, D.C.
30 Bicycle Tours in Wisconsin
25 Mountain Bike Tours in the Adirondacks
25 Mountain Bike Tours in the Hudson Valley
25 Mountain Bike Tours in Massachusetts
25 Mountain Bike Tours in New Jersey
25 Mountain Bike Tours in Vermont
Backroad Bicycling in Connecticut
Backroad Bicycling on Cape Cod, Martha's
   Vineyard, and Nantucket
Backroad Bicycling in Eastern Pennsylvania
The Mountain Biker's Guide to Ski Resorts

Bicycling America's National Parks Series

Bicycling America's National Parks: Arizona &
   New Mexico
Bicycling America's National Parks: California
Bicycling America's National Parks: Oregon &
   Washington
Bicycling America's National Parks: Utah &
   Colorado

We offer many more books on hiking, fly-fishing, travel, nature, and other subjects. Our books are available at bookstores and outdoor stores everywhere. For more information or a free catalog, please call 1-800-245-4151 or write to us at The Countryman Press, P.O. Box 748, Woodstock, Vermont 05091. You can find us on the Internet www.countrymanpress.com.